Her Rite of Passage

Her Rite of Passage

How to Design and Deliver a Rites of Passage Program for African-American Girls and Young Women

Cassandra Mack, MSW

Author of *Smart Moves That Successful Youth Workers Make*
and *Young, Gifted and Doing It: 52 Power Moves for Teens*

Authors Choice Press
New York Lincoln Shanghai

Authors Choice Press
an imprint of iUniverse, Inc.

iUniverse books may be ordered through booksellers or by contacting:

iUniverse
2021 Pine Lake Road, Suite 100
Lincoln, NE 68512
www.iuniverse.com
1-800-Authors (1-800-288-4677)

Because of the dynamic nature of the Internet, any Web addresses
or links contained in this book may have changed
since publication and may no longer be valid.

The views expressed in this work are solely those of the author and do not necessarily
reflect the views of the publisher, and the publisher hereby disclaims
any responsibility for them.

Originally published by Strategies For Empowered Living, Inc.

ISBN: 978-0-595-47036-5

Printed in the United States of America

Table of Contents

Introduction

There is something transformational that occurs when African-American girls and young women come together to learn, share and grow. They discover that they are not alone in their experiences. They also come to find that they have access to a supportive network that can provide them with a sense of sisterhood and community. When carried out successfully, a rites of passage program provides young women with an extended support system, opportunities for growth and development and a forum to develop leadership and life skills. Additionally, it teaches them about traditional African values, principles and practices. An African-centered female rites of passage program not only enables young females who are coming of age to develop into strong, confident young women, it also affirms their sense of identity.

My desire to write *Her Rite of Passage* grew out of my own passage experiences as well as many years of experience developing programs for adolescent girls and young women. In 1993 I developed a girls drop out prevention program for a community-based organization, that later evolved into a rites of passage program. The program was called, Sisters With Choices; and through rituals, educational workshops, journaling, community service, and one-on-one mentoring, Sisters With Choices became a safe haven for adolescent girls and young women to learn, share and grow.

Since the program's inception in 1993, there is no doubt that it has profoundly impacted on the lives of every participant. Some of the girls have gone on to college, while others are building successful careers. Some are still involved in the program as peer leaders, and tutors. In some way, every girl who has passed through the Sisters With Choices program has grown. Whether she has broadened her mental scope, cultivated a supportive network or gained a new perspective on life, the program has evoked, educated, or enlightened each young woman in some way. This is why I believe that there is an undeniable power that occurs when adolescent girls and young women come together to honor their transitional experiences.

Recognizing the power of the rites of passage process, I began to review the literature on female rites programs and studied different program models geared for African-American females between the ages of 12 and 18. I found a great deal of information on rites ceremonies and the historical perspective of the rites of passage process, but there was limited information on how to develop and implement a structured rites of passage program for African-American teenage girls. Thus, *Her Rite of Passage* was born.

Her Rite of Passage is designed to help you develop and deliver a structured rites of passage program for African-American adolescent girls and young women between the ages of 12 and 18. Although the program is designed for African-American girls and young women many of the program components and features can be used as a framework for developing a rites of passage program for young women of any cultural group.

Her Rite of Passage will show you how to:
- Set up a rites of passage program from design to implementation;
- Facilitate and implement the workshop sessions;
- Get buy-in from your organization;
- Recruit participants a.k.a. initiates for your program;
- Recruit volunteers;
- Get parents on board;
- Plan and organize the initiation retreat;
- Plan and organize the crossover ceremony.

In addition, *Her Rite of Passage* will also cover:
- Adolescent female development and the unique issues that impact on African-American teenage girls.
- The special dynamics that occur between African-American daughters and their mothers;
- The impact of the father/daughter relationship on her social and emotional development.

Throughout these pages you will find worksheets, exercises and suggested activities to help you create a solid program. I have provided you with the framework, but it is up to you to make your program work – even if it means making adaptations to suit the needs of your program or conducting additional research in order to become more knowledge about the rites of passage process.

The time has come for women to celebrate and honor one another. It is time for us to reclaim our daughters, whether biological or chosen, and help them to become the confident, empowered young women they were meant to be.

Thank you for choosing *Her Rite of Passage* as your guide. May your journey be a successful and transformational experience.

Peace & Blessings,

Cassandra Mack

1

Celebrating the Passages of Life

Societies have always used some form of ritual or ceremony to mark the passages of life: birth, puberty, marriage, parenthood, advancement to a higher social or religious position, and death. For each of these transitions, there are ceremonies and rituals that recognize and honor the passage from one defined position or stage of life into another. Throughout the world, there are similarities among different cultures in the ceremonies that are used to recognize and honor the various stages that occur over the course of an individual's life cycle. For example, wedding ceremonies are used to honor marriages, baptisms honor spiritual birth or re-birth, birthday celebrations honor a new year of life and funerals honor the life and death of an individual. Although there are differences in how these ceremonies are carried out, the common denominator is, that in just about every culture some form of ritual or ceremony is utilized to mark the many passages of life.

What Is A Rite of Passage?

A rite of passage in its truest sense is the granting of the "right" to pass from one stage of life, development or experience into another. In many cultures, this "right" to passage can only be granted by members of the same cultural group. A rite of passage is marked by the use of ritual and ceremony and signifies that some sort of change or transformation is taking or has taken place.

In many cultures the transition from child to young adult (adolescence) is considered a passage and is marked by the use of ritual and ceremony. In many cultures as a youth progresses through adolescence he/she goes through a series of lessons and initiation activities designed to prepare him/her for adulthood. In many African cultures, when youth reach adolescence they are expected to take on a new role in their community. In order to prepare for their new role, boys and girls are separated from one another, taken out of the village for a specified period of time and are taught life skills, appropriate behaviors, new responsibilities, values and the traditional customs of their culture. When youth successfully complete their training and demonstrate that they understand their new role; they are granted their rites as young adults and a celebration is held in their honor.

Many other cultures formally recognize the transition from child to young adult and consider this transitional stage a passage experience. In the Jewish culture, when a boy reaches adolescence he undergoes a series of lessons designed to prepare him for his new role. Upon successful completion of his study along with other requirements defined by the Jewish culture a Bar mitzvah is held to celebrate his new stage of development. In many Christian cultures when a young person reaches adolescence he/she undergoes an intense Christian study program in order to prepare himself/herself for their new role as a maturing Christian. Upon successful completion of their studies along with other requirements defined by the church, a confirmation is held in their honor.

On many college campuses, sororities and fraternities are considered a rite of passage. When pledging a sorority or fraternity, there is an intense program that pledges must go through as well as a series of initiation activities. Upon successful completion of the organization's requirements, the pledges are granted the right to crossover into the fraternity or sorority.

For many young women from traditional southern cultures, particularly those who come from wealthier or socially connected families, a debutante is considered a rite of passage. The debutante is designed to help young women make a formal debut into southern society. Young women who are being prepared for the debutante receive lessons on social etiquette, appropriate behavior and various other skills that enable them to flourish in well-connected circles.

For many American children and adolescents, the Boy Scouts and Girl Scouts serve as a formal rite of passage. In these organizations youth are taught life skills and the values of the organization. When a youth successfully completes the requirements set by the organization he/she is given a memento to mark their new stage of development and is allowed to move up the ranks.

Most of us have had some sort of rites of passage experience, whether it was being a member of the scouts, being part of a religious program, pledging a fraternity or sorority, joining a fraternal sweetheart club or being part of a structured program that utilized ritual and ceremony to help us move from one level of experience into another.

Using Ceremony and Ritual to Honor Transitions

I believe that ceremony and ritual are powerful ways to honor life changing experiences and developmental milestones. They also deepen our connection to the divine. Through ritual and ceremony we can: acknowledge developmental milestones, honor our individual and collective experiences, celebrate new beginnings, bring closure to endings, celebrate special moments, embrace sacred experiences and release negativity.

Ceremonies and rituals can be created for any occasion: the birth of your rites of passage program, welcoming and honoring parents, volunteers and initiates, recognizing and affirming milestones and achievements, acknowledging the successful completion of your program or any other experience that you want to honor. What is most important is that you are clear about your intention and that the ceremony holds special meaning for those who participate in it. Keep in mind that ceremonies are as diverse as the people who perform and participate in them. This should be taken into consideration whenever you plan to incorporate ceremonies and rituals into your program.

Special rituals and ceremonies are common elements of just about every rites of passage program. They create a sense of solidarity and connection. Since each rites of passage program is unique, I have not prescribed a specific ceremony for you to carry out. Instead, I have provided you with some basic information on common ceremonial tools and I've given you suggested guidelines for carrying out your ceremonies.

Ceremonial Tools

Incense

Incense is used in just about every ceremony. Incense is often used to create a special feeling or energy within the environment by way of smell. Here are some common uses for incense:

- Frankincense – birth, new beginnings, blessings and strength
- Myrrh – birth, new beginnings, purification, healing
- Vanilla - love, light, warmth
- Jasmine – protection, peace and balance
- Musk – strength and love
- Sandalwood – healing
- Rose – love, creativity, happiness

Candles

Candles are often used to symbolize sacredness and add reverence to a ceremony. Candles represent light. They also add beauty and tranquility to the environment. When using candles to perform a ceremony your choice of color is important. Why? Because each color has its' own special meaning.

- <u>White</u> – purity, spirituality and cleansing
- <u>Black</u> – the very beginning, the dawning of something new, creative power, unity
- <u>Green</u> - abundance and success in all areas of life, prosperity renewal, life, healing, and growth
- <u>Yellow</u> – vision, inspiration, motivation, change and creativity
- <u>Red</u> – strength, life, vitality, creativity, and passion
- <u>Brown</u> – centered and grounding
- <u>Orange</u> – action, change
- <u>Pink</u> – love, awakening
- <u>Purple</u> – spirituality, protection, wisdom, the highest spiritual color

Bells

Bells are used during ceremonies to signify the start of something new, and to let people know that it's time to come together. During the commencement of your crossover ceremony or at any specified time during your ceremony, you can ring a bell to indicate that the ceremony or a particular ritual is about to begin. Bells are used frequently in religious ceremonies. Bells are not a necessary component for your rites of passage ceremonies, but they do add a nice element.

Drums

In many African, Latin and Native American ceremonies, drums are used to intensify the ceremony. Drums can be used for a specific dance ritual, meditation or any other aspect of your ceremony that you wish to enhance with percussive sound.

Music and Song

Music is believed by many to be the universal language that unites us all. Through music and song you can give praise, convey gratitude, love, happiness, closure, and any other feeling that you wish to express. When using music, make sure that your selections are appropriate for your overall purpose and relevant to your ceremonial theme.

Dance

Dance is used in many ceremonies to express a variety of emotions and themes. In many African, Native American, Latin and Asian cultures dance is used to worship, give thanks and celebrate special occasions. When incorporating dance into your rites program, make sure that the dance is not merely a form of entertainment but an expression of creativity and sacredness.

Clothing

When carrying out ceremonies, it is a good idea to wear special attire that is reserved just for these ceremonies. You can elect to have a specific color scheme like white, purple or any other color that holds special meaning for the group. You can also choose to wear traditional African clothing complimented by a gele (head wrap). Clothes should be comfortable and loose so that everyone can move around with ease. You can fundraise in order to purchase special attire, or you can find out if any of the initiates or parents sew and create your own outfits.

Kwanzaa Symbols

Kwanzaa is a special holiday that pays tribute to the cultural roots of people of African ancestry. Kwanzaa means the first or the first fruits of the harvest, in the East African language of Kiswahili. We will discuss the principles of Kwanzaa and how to incorporate them into your rites program as we move along in the guidebook. Like many holidays, Kwanzaa has its own unique symbols that represent and reinforce African principles, concepts and traditional practices. Following are the seven basic symbols of Kwanzaa. By incorporating these symbols into your rites program, participants will learn about sacred objects that reflect the life and struggle of people of African ancestry.

1. **Mazao** – (fruit and vegetables) since Kwanzaa means "first fruits", the mazao is significant because they symbolize the rewards of collective labor.
2. **Mkeka** – (place mat) the mkeka is the symbol of tradition and history. It represents the sharing of the harvest and maintains unity in the family by encouraging families to eat together.
3. **Kinara** – (the seven place candle holder, one black, three red and three green) The Kinara is used to symbolize the continental Africans, or ancestors.
4. **Vibunzi** – (ears of corn) The Vibunzi represents children. Traditionally each family uses an ear of corn to represent each child. For your rites program you can use an ear of corn to represent each initiate with special emphasis on the importance of producing good fruit such as: giving back to the community, using their talents to make the world a better place, respecting themselves and others, having an attitude of gratitude or any other principle that promotes productivity.
5. **Zawadi** – (gifts) Zawadi are gifts that are given to reinforce personal growth and reward the initiates' commitment and excellence. Zawadi are not given automatically, but they are based on the individual having earned them. Zawadi is not based on commercialism but comes from the heart so they do not have to be costly. Homemade gifts, books, journals, and keepsakes are strongly encouraged.
6. **Kikombe Cha Umoja** – (the communal unity cup) the communal unity cup symbolizes the first principle of Kwanzaa, unity. It is filled with water and used to pour libation in remembrance of the ancestors, and anyone in the group's family who has passed on. If the group wishes, the unity cup can be passed among members of the group and a sipping gesture can be made to promote the spirit of unity.

7. **<u>Mishumaa Saba</u>** – (the seven candles) the Mishumaa Saba represent Nguzo Saba, the seven principles of Kwanzaa. Each candle represents a distinct principle of Nguzo Saba beginning with the black center candle to represent unity. After the unity (umoja) candle is lit all the other candles are lit from left to right. The lighting of the Mishumaa Saba is generally conducted on the seventh day of Kwanzaa, however you can make adaptations and incorporate the lighting of the Mishumaa Saba in the final ritual of your rites of passage crossover ceremony.

Incorporating the Elements Into Your Rituals and Ceremonies

When performing a ceremony, you can use the elements to enhance the positive focus of your program. The four elements are representative of what we need to survive and sustain ourselves. Just as you would use man made tools to heighten the experience of those participating in the ceremony, it is desirable to use nature's elements for additional purifying benefits.

- <u>Earth</u> – Earth is the grounding force, which brings forth life. Biblical scripture teaches that we were made from earth and to earth we shall return. In your ceremonies you can incorporate soil or sea salt to represent the earth's wisdom, purity and power to produce life.
- <u>Water</u> – water is the sustaining element for all living things. It is cleansing, healing, and purifying. It is fluid and always in motion. It can change form. You can use water for libation, purifying and just about any ritual performed in your ceremony.
- <u>Fire</u> – fire is a powerful element that symbolizes passion for life, vitality, warmth, creativity and purification. If at all possible you can perform a special ceremony just for initiates around a campfire. You can have each initiate write down a goal that she wants to accomplish and have her toss the paper into the fire with adult supervision to symbolize the creative spark or to signify her burning passion to achieve the goal. Or, if there is a troubling issue that an initiate is dealing with, you can ask her to say a silent prayer and make a tossing gesture into the campfire to represent that she is letting go of the issue. This is a very powerful activity that may bring up strong feelings. Make sure to have trained adults on hand to deal with any emotional issues that may arise.
- <u>Air</u> – air is the breath of life. Air symbolizes breath and breath symbolizes life. You can lead the group in a guided breathing exercise by becoming very conscious of your breathing and encouraging participants to do the same. While saying an affirmation or leading the group through a creative visualization exercise you can incorporate conscious breathing.

Incorporating Prayer and Meditation Into Your Rituals and Ceremonies

Before incorporating prayer and meditation into your rites program, you need to find out what your organization's policies are around the use of prayer and meditation, and then use your judgment when approaching these issues. Keep in mind that prayer and meditation are almost always incorporated into the African-centered rites of passage program and if you take these elements out, then you are not staying true to the cultural base of the program.

Traditionally, for people of African ancestry, prayer has been an integral part of social and family life. Prayer is communion with God. It's taking time out to talk with and listen to the Creator. Prayer allows us to seek God's guidance and grace, give thanks, release heavy emotional issues, and talk about whatever is in our hearts.

Since you will probably have young women of different faiths and beliefs participating in your program, it is important that the prayers you incorporate are non-denominational, unless you are leading a denomination-specific rites of passage program. You can ask each initiate to say her own prayer out loud or silently. You can also create your own prayer with the group giving thanks, asking for guidance and clarity; then you can close the prayer by asking for God's grace. You can pray standing, sitting, lying down or kneeling. You can pray for yourself and for others. You can pray during the beginning, middle or end of your ceremonies. You can pray during all of your ceremonies or just during the crossover ceremony. It's totally up to you.

Meditation is another important element of the African-centered rites of passage program. Meditation is the process of being still and getting quiet in order to reflect, receive and renew. Meditation clears the mind and opens the heart. It relaxes the body and calms the spirit. When you meditate or lead a group in meditation you should have a clear purpose, which could be relaxation, peace, release, or enlightenment.

If you and your initiates have difficulty being still and clearing your mind of all thoughts, then the best starting place for your group would be relaxation meditation. You can sit in a comfortable chair, with your back straight, feet flat on the floor and arms gently at your sides. While in this position, close your eyes, take a deep breath and relax your body. If you have difficulty becoming still and relaxing your body, talk to yourself. Say, " *I am clearing my mind of all thoughts.*" " *My body is beginning to relax.*" If the participants are having difficulty becoming still, say " *You are clearing your mind of all thoughts.*" "*Your body is beginning to relax.*"

Keep in mind that prayer and meditation should never be forced on the group. If you have initiates who are uncomfortable with prayer and meditation, then they should always have the right to pass.

Using ritual and ceremony to honor transitional experiences is a sacred undertaking. As you lead initiates through various rituals and ceremonies, it is important that both you and the initiates prepare yourselves mentally, emotionally and physically for the sacredness of what you are about to do. Here are some suggestions for preparing yourself and others for rituals and ceremonies.

- *Go In With An Open Heart and A Positive Frame of Mind*

Whenever you are about to participate in a ceremony, it is important that you start out with a positive frame of mind. Our attitude pervades the space within and around us. The spirit of your ceremony can be greatly hampered if you or anyone else goes in with an angry, unwilling, impatient or negative attitude of any kind.

- *Go In With A Clean Body and A Clear Head*

They very act of cleansing the body and clearing the mind of all toxins is a purification process. It is key that you communicate to everyone who is involved in your rites program the importance of being clean and sober before participating in any ceremony. Purification is the process of washing away any barriers that prevent us from tapping our inner power and manifesting our unlimited potential. This is why sobriety and cleanliness are important.

- *Bless Your Ceremonial Environment*

Blessing is the act of using prayer to create a positive environment and sacred situation. It is taking some time out before you actually begin the ceremony to seek God's protection and grace as well as honor the situation or the environment. It is a good idea to bless your environment before the other participants arrive, so that you can set positive spiritual energy into motion before the ceremony actually begins. This way if people come in with a negative attitude, you would have already protected yourself, your initiates and your ceremony from their negative energy.

- *Talk to Participants to Get A Sense of How They Feel About Participating In Ceremonies and Rituals*

As mentioned earlier, using ritual and ceremony to honor transformational experiences is a sacred undertaking. Therefore it is important to get a sense of how initiates feel about participating in this aspect of your rites program. You may have some people who are comfortable and excited by the idea, while others may feel uncomfortable or uncertain about participating in ceremonies and rituals. As the program leader you will have to find a way to help those who are uncomfortable gain comfort. One of the best ways to do this is to find out what aspect of the ceremony makes them feel uneasy or alienated, then explain the purpose of that particular part of the ceremony. If this does not work you can also ask participants to offer suggestions, and incorporate their ideas into your rites ceremonies. However, if a participant's suggestion is contrary to the message and feeling that you want to convey in your ceremony then you have the right to decline the suggestion. And if there is an aspect of your ceremony that goes against an initiate's beliefs then she has the right to pass. In the end you and the other program leaders will have to decide which parts of the program are absolutely essential and which parts need to be negotiated.

- *Help Participants to Make the Connection Between Ceremony and Their Life Experiences*

Before you begin any ceremony, take time out to explain the significance of the ceremony. If there are tools or terms that members are unfamiliar with, explain why and how they are being used. After every ceremony allow time for debriefing. Debriefing is the process of helping group members understand why a particular exercise, activity or ritual is being used and how it applies to a particular aspect of their lives or their day-to-day experiences.

- *Know Your Organization's Culture and Constraints*

Just like people, every organization has a culture. Every organization has its own way of doing things and expects the people who are employed by them to follow suit. Due to your organization's culture and, or policies you may not be able to include all of the ceremonial tools and methods into your rites program. If this is the case, then the challenge for you is to find a way to make adjustments in your program, while remaining authentic to African-based principles, practices and values.

Clarifying Your Motivation

Before you set out to design your rites of passage program, it is a good idea to get clear about why you want to offer a rites of passage program for African-American young women in the first place. What is your motivation for wanting to develop a rites of passage program for African-American females? Do you believe that the African-American females in your agency are underserved? Do you believe that the African-American females in your organization or community are not being serviced in a culturally competent manner? Are you responding to a grant that was made available for those servicing African-American females? Are you looking to offer a more African-centered approach to your youth programs?

The clearer and more explicit you are about what you want to offer and why, the better able you will be to decide, in advance how to best design and deliver your program. Just as if you were thinking about planting a garden, first you would need to decide what kind of plant life you want to grow. Then you would need to figure out how much work the garden would entail. Looking beforehand at what you need to do to get your garden into full bloom will help you develop the most appropriate plan for cultivating your garden. This same principle applies to your rites of passage program. For example, if you just sent out fliers inviting young women and their parents to a rites of passage orientation without being clear about why you were starting the program, what the purpose was, and what you were going to offer; you would probably have difficulty getting people to participate in and support your program. Why? Because they wouldn't be clear about what you were offering and why.

What Kind of Seeds Do You Want to Plant In Your Garden?

To assist you in getting a clearer picture of what you want to offer and why, I offer the following questions for you to consider.

1. What is prompting you to do this? What is motivating you to want to start a rites of passage program?

_____

_____

2. What kind of rites of passage program do you want to offer?

_____

_____

3. Were you ever involved in a structured rites of passage program? If yes, what was that experience like for you? If no, what informal rites of passage experiences have you had?

_____

_____

4. Do you feel drawn to offer this program at the organization that you work for, or will the program operate independent of your organization?

_____

_____

5. If you offer the program at your organization how will you work within your organization's guidelines without compromising the cultural integrity of the program?

_____

_____

6. If you offer the program independent of your organization, how will you ensure that you are providing the highest quality of service for your program participants?

_____

_____

7. What purpose and need will your rites of passage program serve?

_____

_____

8. What do you want young women to get out of your program?

_____

_____

9. What are your requirements for initiates?

_____

_____

10. What are your requirements for volunteers and staff?

_____

_____

11. What are your requirements for the program? What is a must? What's nice but cannot be realistically carried out at this time?

_____

_____

12.What kind of things do you want to avoid in your program?

_____

_____

The answers to these questions should help you become clearer about your motivation for wanting to offer this rites of passage program.

Once you begin to get a clearer picture of what's motivating you, start talking about the program with friends, colleagues and peers. Ask for their honest feedback and support. Their feedback will provide you with information about people's familiarity with the African-centered rites of passage process and their receptiveness to it.

As you begin to think about how you want to carry out your rites of passage program, you may start to notice that you are moving into a new realm of experience, which in essence is the start of your own passage experience. Your rites of passage program will bring many opportunities for change, which can be very frightening. With transformation we step into unchartered territories, where everything both magnificent and terrifying is possible. But when you remain open to change and committed to excellence, you will have the seeds to sow a successful rites of passage program.

2

Why A Rites of Passage Program for African-American Girls?

Why a rites of passage program for African-American girls and young women? Because African-American girls face greater challenges than females of any other ethnic group. And as a result, they need programs that are designed with their unique challenges in mind and that address their needs in a culturally competent manner. Here are some of the challenges that African-American girls and young women face:

- According to the Center for Disease Control, African-American females between the ages 14 and 25 have the highest incidence of HIV and AIDS.
- African-American girls are three times as likely as White girls and twice as likely as Latina girls to have had some form of sexual intercourse by age 13.
- According to the Bureau of Justice Statistics, African-American girls are twice as likely as their White counterparts to be the victims of crime.
- African-American females are the fastest growing prison population.
- African-American girls are twice as likely as White girls to be overweight and to suffer health problems resulting from their weight.
- According to the American Bar Association, delinquency cases involving African-American girls rose 106 percent from 1988 to 1997 compared with a 74 percent rise among White girls.

While many African-American women have excelled beyond their wildest dreams and knocked down doors at the highest level of achievement like Oprah Winfrey, Condoleezza Rice and Venus and Serena Williams, we must still recognize that African-American young women of this generation are grappling with issues and challenges that the generations before them did not have to deal with or at least not with the same level of severity. And this is the stage of life where they should be preparing for their future and having fun; not raising children, managing a life with HIV, worrying about their safety at school or carrying heavy emotional baggage because they come from fragmented families.

A history of oppression and injustice compounded by the perpetual fragmentation of the Black family has caused many African-American youth to lose sight of who they are as well as the value-system that has enabled the generations that came before them to survive and thrive in spite of their harsh circumstances. It has placed additional emotional stressors on far too many Black youth, both male and female who have never known the sense of family that comes from being raised in a two-parent household or at least by having a loving relationship with both parents. When we consider the impact of the breakdown of the family, a failing school system, a society obsessed with sex and materialism, the objectification of African-American women in music videos and print media and a growing prison industry designed to warehouse young people rather than help integrate them back into society; it's no wonder that so many African-American young women are in crisis. Traditionally, African-Americans have been a people of faith, action, determination, creativity, community and humanity. But many of us are so disconnected from our cultural umbilical cord that the very things that centered and connected us are now undervalued or not important at all.

In my seminar work with African–American girls and young women, I frequently ask them to share their feelings about life, love, family, education, careers, spirituality and the future. A handful of young women from each group discuss the importance of God, family, education, giving back to the community, love, respect and a sense of hope for the future. But the overwhelming majority shared some things that were quite disturbing. Many said that they had poor relationships with their parents. Some did not know who their fathers were and if they did they had little or no contact with them. Many believed that hard work and a good education does not pay off anymore. Those who had children had strained relationships with their child's father. While others seem to think of abortion as a method of birth control. Some had a little bit of faith in Black males, while others thought that all men were dogs. Many felt that they did not have anyone they could talk to about their innermost thoughts and feelings. Some were able to count on one hand the number of sexual partners they've had, while others were too embarrassed to disclose. And there were a few who were virgins. Some were having sexual relationships with men who were ten and twenty years their senior. Some could not think of at least one person in their family who achieved a measure of success.

So the question remains, Why a rites of passage program for African-American adolescent girls and young women? Because we cannot let despair and indifference be their only voice. As adults who have a sincere and vested interest in helping African-American girls grow into strong, emotionally healthy young women, we must help them get back to the truth of who they are – bright, capable and resilient young women. The African-centered rites of passage program provides African-American girls with many of the tools they need to grow into strong, emotionally healthy young women such as: a sense of history as African-American young women, coping strategies to better deal with sexism and racism, life skills that will enable them to become successfully self-sufficient, values that promote good decisions, a support system and a sense of identity and self-worth. I have found that African-American girls who participate in structured rites of passage programs typically do better than those who do not.

The Benefits of An African-centered Rites Program

How do African-American girls and young women benefit from an African-centered rites of passage program? Following are some of the benefits:

- *It builds self-worth and a sense of identity.*

Besides preparing youth to make the successful passage into adulthood, one of the primary goals of the African-centered rites of passage program is to build self-worth and instill a sense of identity in African-American youth. During slavery the names (cultural identity) and rights (freedom, human value) of African-Americans were taken away. Having your identity stolen from you and your freedom taken away will no doubt take its toll on your self-esteem. And although African-Americans are no longer physically enslaved, many are still dealing with the emotional and psychological ramifications that slavery and disenfranchisement have left behind. The African-centered rites of passage program addresses this issue by instilling cultural pride and a sense of identity among African-American youth, for the purposes of this book, young women.

- *It instills a sense of family and unity.*

During and after slavery it was the communal support of the sisterhood that enabled African-American women to survive and overcome their harsh conditions in order to create a better future for the generations to come. African-American women of the older generations knew that belittling each other, hoarding resources or allowing philosophical differences to divide them would be detrimental to the survival of African-American people as a whole. Yet today many African-American young women do not trust or even like each other and as a result are not only disconnected from their biological families, but from the family of sisterhood as well.

In the African-centered rites of passage program the principle of Umoja is taught to all initiates. Umoja *(unity)* is the first principle of Kwanzaa. It teaches that African-Americans should strive for and maintain unity in the family, community, nation and race. Africans are a communal people and have traditionally believed that spiritually and culturally all people of African ancestry are family. This is why many African-Americans refer to one another as brother and sister. The rites of passage program addresses this issue by providing young women with an extended family of initiates and mentors.

- *Provides African-American young women with a deeper connection to their history and traditional way of life.*

Many African-American youth are disconnected from their history and traditional way of life. Because many African-American youth have little or no knowledge of their cultural heritage, they often do not understand the significance of their ancestors' struggle and how this struggle has afforded them the rights they have today. Some African-Americans choose to forget their history and surrender their ancestral way of life in favor of a more Euro-centric value system and worldview. When people lose their sense of cultural ancestry, self-hatred begins to replaces self-love and cultural shame replaces cultural pride. The ramifications of alienation and cultural disconnection are apparent when we witness African-American youth disrespecting adults, or barely pubescent girls trying to emulate the scantily dressed young women in the music videos, or when we hear a rapper rapping about committing a homicide with the insensitivity of swatting a fly. When alienation and disconnection permeate the consciousness of our Black youth, the implications are lethal. And in case you are in doubt just go back to the challenges that African-American girls face that I presented earlier.

As adults who have a sincere interest in helping African-American girls become strong, emotionally healthy young women, we need to help African-American girls embrace their history and develop a healthy appreciation for their traditional way of life. Since they are both African and American, we need to help them realize that they can embrace what's African without denouncing what's American. The African-centered rites of passage program is a wonderful way to introduce young women to traditional African principles and practices as well as teach them about African-American history.

- *It provides young women with a sense of belonging*

During adolescence peer relationships become increasingly important. And during the teen years peer acceptance takes precedence over adult approval. Teens want to belong. Because of their need to belong, adolescents, for the purposes of this book, adolescent girls, are at a greater risk of giving into negative peer pressure. The African-centered rites of passage program meets their need for belonging by providing them with a structured, positive peer group to belong to.

- *It provides young women with a safe-haven to address critical social issues and develop life skills*

Girls and young women are growing up in a time where they have to deal with many issues that you and I probably never had to face. In my generation the worst fear was getting pregnant. Many girls of today's generation fear much worse fates such as; contracting HIV or AIDS, being the victim of gang violence or violence in school, or getting caught in a crossfire shooting. Today more than ever girls need their own space where they can talk about issues that affect their lives in order to come up with real life management strategies. The group rap sessions provide girls with practical strategies for dealing with tough life issues.

- *It provides young women with one-to-one mentoring.*

In my first book, *Smart Moves That Successful Youth Workers Make*, I discuss the importance of youth workers serving as mentors to young people. Effective mentoring is the act of supporting a young person and becoming part of his/her support system so that he/she can come to you for guidance and encouragement. When a girl has a mentor as part of her supportive network, she has a special person in her life who she can talk to and look up to.

An integral part of the African-centered female rites of passage program is the mentoring relationship. Each initiate is paired up with a mentor who guides and encourages her, usually for the duration of the rites program. However, many girls stay in contact with their mentors long after they crossover.

- *It instills morals and builds integrity*

Today's youth receive so many conflicting messages regarding how to succeed and get ahead, that it's no wonder that many are so misguided. On one hand, they are told to work hard, get an education, be honest and it will all pay off in the long run. But on the other hand, they see people who are corrupt and dishonest succeed and get ahead. It is important that young people learn how to live with integrity and to make morally sound decisions. The African-centered rites of passage program helps to instill morals and build integrity in youth by teaching them the code of MAAT, which we will discuss later in the book, and the principles of Nguzo Saba, which are the principles commonly associated with Kwanzaa.

- *It formally recognizes a girl's transition from child to young woman.*

By way of the crossover ceremony, a rites of passage program formally recognizes a girl's transition into womanhood and it honors her new role in the community.

The Different Types of African-centered Rites of Passage Programs

African-centered rites of passage programs are sprouting up just about everywhere. As African-Americans develop a growing hunger for a deeper connection to their ancestral way of life, and seek culturally competent ways to position Black youth for success, more and more are turning to the structured rites of passage process. There are different types of African-centered rites programs that utilize a combination of African-based principles, practices and customs. Following is a sampler of the different types of rites of passage programs being carried out by African-Americans. It is a good idea to review them in order to get a better sense of the type of program that you'd like to offer.

- ### Church Based Rites of Passage Programs
  African-centered rites of passage programs are being sponsored by churches such as the Abyssinian Baptist Church in Harlem, New York, Allen AME church in Queens, New York and the Wheeler Avenue Baptist church in Texas. The Church is the oldest and largest institution in the African-American community. Not only was the church a safe haven for escaped slaves during slavery, and the primary meeting place for those involved in the civil rights movement, it was also the place where African-Americans worshiped together and educated their children.

  Since Black churches are primarily led by African-Americans, the benefit is that you will be able to remain true to the cultural base of your program. Many church based rites of passage programs use the Bible as their foundation. They also incorporate prayer, scriptural reading and religious music into their rites programs. The major benefits of church based rites of passage programs are: you do not have to sell the program to the church because many are familiar with the rites of passage process and you do not have to look far to find sponsors, mentors and initiates because you can usually find them in the church.

- ### Home Based Rites of Passage Programs
  Home based rites of passage programs are usually made up of female friends or family members who want to offer their teenage daughters or the adolescent girls in their neighborhood a structured rites of passage experience. There are many African-centered rites of passage programs being carried out in the homes of parents and other caring adults. One such group is Sisters Saving Sisters, which is made up of seven women and their daughters. This group meets twice a month and they take turns leading educational workshops, and facilitating activities. The book *Transformation* by Mafori Moore describes a similar process of

friends coming together to create a structured rites of passage program for their daughters.

The major benefits of a home based rites of passage program are: like-minded women come together for the purpose of nurturing African-American girls, the informal tone allows for more freedom to run the program the way you see fit and since participants share similar beliefs and values you do not have to sell the program as much as you would if you offered it at an organization. The major drawback is, since you are operating as an independent group, you may have greater difficulty obtaining funding and corporate donations as well as getting volunteers to support your program.

- **Private Rites of Passage Programs**

Private rites of passage programs are programs that are carried out by individuals who are consultants or who have small businesses and offer rites of passage programs and activities as part of their business. Unlike home based programs where a group of women come together to offer a rites of passage program right from their home, individuals who offer a private rites of passage program are usually trained professionals who work with groups on a paid consultative basis or they rent a space, market to the public and charge a fee. Author and holistic health practitioner Queen Affua offers a rites of passage program called, Sacred Women. Her program is based on Egyptology and traditional African principles.

- **Seminar and Convention Sponsored Rites of Passage Programs**

Seminar or convention sponsored rites of passage programs are just what they sound like, rites programs that are sponsored by seminar or convention companies. At the African-American Women on Tour Convention three three-day rites of passage programs are offered: one for teenage girls, one for young women, and one for adult women. These programs utilize ritual, meditation, and libation. Seminar and convention sponsored rites of passage programs offer a condensed version of the traditional African-centered rites program.

- **Agency and Professional Association Sponsored Rites of Passage Programs**

As the structured rites of passage process gains more notoriety, more and more organizations are utilizing this process as a tool to prepare youth for successful independent living. Many youth service agencies and professional associations like the National Association of Black Social Workers are sponsoring rites of passage programs for young people. The advantages of the agency and professional association sponsored rites of passage program are organizational support and greater access to resources. The drawbacks are: organizational constraints, office politics and having to sell the program to administrators who are not familiar with the African-centered rites of passage process.

As you can see there are many different kinds of African-centered rites of passage programs. Rites programs are as diverse as the people who conduct and participate in them. The challenge for you is, to figure out what type of rites program you want to offer and weigh the benefits and drawbacks in order to offer the kind of program that is most suited to your goals and needs.

3

Young, Black and Female

What does it mean to be young, Black, and female in today's society? Perhaps this sounds like a strange question, but if you are going to offer a rites of passage program to African-American girls and young women, then you need to understand who they are and how they view the world. This is not to say that all African-American females share the same values, beliefs, and worldview, because there are always exceptions. What this means is, there are some similarities with respect to the cultural orientation and socialization process that African-Americans "generally" bring with them.

Following are guidelines designed to provide you with a framework for understanding the cultural orientation and socialization process of African-Americans. Keep in mind that the guidelines are "general" points to be considered and will not apply to all African-Americans.

Gaining A Better Understanding of the Cultural and Social Orientation of African-Americans

- **Extended kinships are vital.**

  In Dr. Jerome Schiele's book, *Human Services and the Afrocentric Paradigm*, he indicates that in traditional African society extended kinships created a climate that encouraged the sharing of resources and land. In traditional African society, people did not view themselves as isolated entities, but as part of an extended family. This extended family provided people with a sense of belonging and group cohesiveness. Even today, it is not uncommon for people of African ancestry to create kinship ties with people they are not biologically related to.

- **Individual and group responsibility are mutually dependent**

  In traditional African society, individual and group responsibility are viewed as mutually dependent. Success of one belongs to the entire group and if one succeeded he or she was expected to give back to the community. For example, when Jackie Robinson became the first African-American baseball player to play for an all White team, his success was viewed as an achievement for the entire African-American community.

- **In the African-American community there are clear lines of demarcation that distinguish people according to age, social position and life experience.**

    Historically, in the African-American community there are clear lines of demarcation that distinguish people according to age, social position and life experience. For example, youth are not afforded the same rights and privileges as adults and they are expected to give adults a certain level of respect. Clergy are given a different level of respect than lay people and individuals who are in high social positions are often given a certain level of respect based on their position. An example of how the lines of demarcation are evident in the African-American community is the custom of referring to elders by their last name or by saying sir or ma'am. Although much of this tradition has changed, honoring boundaries is still viewed as a sign of respect in the African-American community.

- **Affirmation of self comes from connection to God, knowledge of self and connection to family.**

    In traditional African culture, affirmation of self is an internal experience. Historically, our self worth was not connected to our net worth, stature in life, educational accomplishments or the achievement of external accolades. Instead, it came from our connection to God, knowledge and love of self and our ties to family. In American culture, affirmation of self is often based on external factors such as: social position, economic status, physical attractiveness and other external accolades.

    This is not to say that the identity of the African-American young woman is never impacted by or based on external factors. It means that by nature of her socialization and cultural orientation she tends to have a more internal view of herself. This is why there is such a hunger in the African-American community for images that represent the wide spectrum of African-American culture and traditional way of life. One of your tasks as a rites of passage leader is to help the girls in your program find positive images that affirm who they are and acknowledge their strengths and attributes.

- **Traditionally, African-Americans are a faith-based people.**

    During and after slavery the Black church was central to the progress and advancement of people of African ancestry. It was a refuge for freedom fighters and escaped slaves. It was a meeting place for civil rights activists. Historically, it was the center for social and political change in the African-American community.

    Traditionally, whenever there was a crisis that occurred in an African-American family, the preacher not the therapist was sought out for guidance and support and the elders came together to pray. For the most part this is still true today. In the ancient African religion of Yoruba, it is believed that all human beings are a divine expression of the Creator and if we practice the spiritual principles of truth, order, justice, faith and patience we will reap positive spiritual and physical results. It is this recognition of and relationship to the divine that has enabled African-Americans to survive and overcome the harshest and most inhumane of circumstances. If you are to work with African-American girls in a culturally competent manner you must give them room in your program to honor their spirituality.

- **Feelings of inadequacy, oppression and injustice must not be ignored or minimized they must be addressed and openly discussed.**

Depending on the group that you are servicing, some of the females in your program will be the first in their families to go to college and gain access to resources that their mothers and grandmothers did not have access to. But this does not mean that they will not be subjected to or affected by oppression and injustice. Although this generation of African-American young women have rights and privileges that their foremothers did not have, you cannot forget that they are still the descendents of a people who were taken from their land, stripped of their culture, and robbed of their humanity. They are still products of a system that was built on white male supremacy, which has had a trickling impact on not only their psyche, but also on how others perceive and treat them.

Although African-Americans have come a long way, they still have a long way to go. With this in mind, it is important that when African-American females tell you about incidents that they perceive as racist, sexist and unjust that you do not undermine the validity of their feelings, or tell them that they are being overly sensitive or give them a list of reasons to justify the other person's behavior. Instead, just listen empathically and assist them in developing strategies for dealing with racist and sexist remarks and behavior.

- **There is a shift from traditional African values to New Jack values**

In Dr. Jawanza Kunjufu's book, *Hip-Hop vs. MAAT: A Psycho/Social Analysis of Values*, he suggests that this generation of youth specifically African-Americans are moving away from the traditional values of MAAT and Nguzo Saba (we will discuss these in detail later in the book) and are adopting New Jack values, which are values commonly associated with rap music and Hip Hop culture, specifically gangsta rap. These values are: materialism, profit, sex, individualism and aggression. However, if you look at the values that are emphasized by the larger society, you will notice that the values coined as New Jack are the same values that are reinforced by the Eurocentric (mainstream) worldview. In an article written for the Journal of Black Studies in 1984 by Dr. Na'im Akbar entitled *Afrocentric Social Science for Human Liberation,* Akbar indicates that unlike the Afrocentric paradigm in the Eurocentric paradigm individualism and capitalism are emphasized. If individualism and capitalism are emphasized by our society particularly in the media and today's youth are constantly tuned into the media, then it would be safe to say that young people will be impacted by the images that they see and hear.

What does this mean for you as a rites of passage facilitator? It means that you need to find creative ways to help the young women you work with move away from New Jack values in order to incorporate more traditional African values into their lives. One way to do this is to use rap music and hip hop culture as a tool to address critical social issues that impact your initiates, then help them utilize traditional African values to manage these issues.

As mentioned earlier the guidelines presented are general points to keep in mind. The guidelines should not take the place of you conducting additional research on how to work with young women of African ancestry. They are offered to help you gain a better understanding of the "general" social realities and cultural orientation of African-Americans.

A Primer on African-American Female Development

What is it about the developmental process of African-American adolescent girls that is different from girls of other ethnicities? Two things: the cultural orientation that they bring to the developmental process and the social factors that impact on their development. Adolescence is a stage of development where a child begins to transition into a young adult. During this stage, the primary task of the adolescent is to establish her own identity and to find her place in the world. For African-American females, this task is compounded, because they very nature of self is called into question. Being both African and American there is a struggle to embrace both identities and bridge both worlds.

During adolescence it is part of the natural developmental process for adolescents, for the purposes of this book, adolescent girls, to take greater risks, defy the rules, seek acceptance from their peers and reject the status quo. As a girl moves through adolescence, she will progress through three stages: early adolescence which usually occurs between the ages of 11-13 and sometimes a little younger, middle adolescence which usually occurs between the ages of 14-16 and late adolescence which begins at 17 and ends at 21. With each of these stages there are targeted areas of growth that form the foundation for the progression into the next stage. Keep in mind that every girl will move through each stage at a different pace. Some will progress earlier, while others will develop at later intervals. The information that follows on African-American female development is meant to be a general guide, not a rigid measuring stick. With the exception of menstruation and other gender specific physical characteristics, males move through the same developmental stages as females, but for the purposes of this book we will focus solely on female development.

Early Adolescence

Physically, a girl's body begins to change and she will experience the most rapid growth since her newborn and pre-school years. Her childlike body begins to transform into a body that is capable of reproduction. She will experience changes in height and weight and the first pubic hairs may appear. Her breast will begin to grow and become more round and her nipples will begin to project outward. At this stage she may experience spotting or a full menstruation may occur. Some of her physiological changes will occur before menstruation, others occur during and after the onset of menses. More than any other physiological change, menstruation marks the beginning of womanhood.

Intellectually, the early adolescent female has expanded capabilities for abstract thinking. She is beginning to connect choices to their consequences, but she is still growing in this area and will need help in learning how to make good decisions. Research shows that in junior high and high school, girls have a tendency to decline in academic performance and motivation because they become more interested in socializing. Research also shows that during this time teachers have a tendency of calling on boys and responding more favorably than they do with girls when boys respond with correct answers. In order to facilitate healthy intellectual development, you should encourage initiates to: embrace learning for the sake of learning, participate more in class and discover what excites, motivates, and challenges them.

Emotionally, the early adolescent female experiences a multitude of emotions often resulting from the physical changes that she is experiencing. During this stage, she is capable of expressing multiple emotions in a short period of time. She may be happy and enthusiastic one minute and irritable and grouchy the next. Early adolescent females often become focused on their biological changes and may withdraw or act out because of their own self-consciousness or because of the way others respond to them. In order to foster healthy emotional development during early adolescence you can encourage initiates to talk about their feelings and experiences and help them learn effective ways to manage their feelings.

Morally, the early adolescent female begins to think about fairness, justice and morality. She will begin to ask questions around social issues in order to develop a clearer picture of what's right and what's wrong. Because she is still growing in this area, she will more than likely base her decisions on what the majority of her peers are doing instead of her own set of values. This is why it is important that your rites program helps initiates adopt values that lead to ethical choices.

Socially, the early adolescent female is pulling away from her parents and the other adults in her life in order to form a sense of self and develop closer relationships with peers. Parents may feel uncomfortable with their daughters' new attitude so you may need to reassure them that pulling way from parents is a normal part of adolescent development. You may also notice that during early adolescence most girls prefer to hang out with each other, but many will express a romantic interest in males. As a rites of passage facilitator you can use this as an opportunity to discuss positive female friendships and healthy male/female relationships.

Middle Adolescence

Physically, the middle adolescent female body is closer to that of an adult. Physical growth begins to slow down during this stage. Body fat increases around her hips, thighs, calves and breasts and her pelvic region increases in width. She begins to look less like a girl and more like a woman. As she begins to look more like a woman, she may receive wanted and unwanted attention from older males. You will need to talk with her about how to appropriately handle this attention as well as what to do when adult males come on too strong or behave in ways that make her feel uncomfortable. You will also need to talk to them about the common ploys that older males use to initiate sexual relationships with young girls.

Intellectually, the capacity for abstract thinking increases even more. She understands that there are consequences to her choices. She is still attempting to establish an identity apart from her family. No longer a child, but not quite a woman she searches, questions and retreats in order to begin to answer the question, "Who am I?" In order to answer this question, it is important that African-American young women, have access to images that embrace and affirm their identity as African-Americans and as young women.

Emotionally, the middle adolescent female has an increased sense of self-awareness, and autonomy, but she still leans on family and other trusted adults for guidance and support. During this stage, she may begin to test the limits and question parental authority. This will probably present a challenge for many African-American parents, because honor and respect for elders is part of the traditional value system. This goes back to the clear lines of demarcation in the African-American community that I presented earlier. When these lines are crossed, power struggles between parents, especially mothers and daughters, are likely to occur.

Morally, the middle adolescent female will watch you and other influential adults and look for inconsistencies between what adults say and what they actually do. She is becoming clearer about her values and forming stronger opinions about what's right and what's wrong. The African-American female will begin to look at what's happening on the home front, in her community and society at large and will notice that race and gender affect just about every aspect of American life, particularly access to accurate information and equal resources. She will begin to raise questions and may look to you for a moral explanation.

Socially, the middle adolescent female is more selective when it comes to forming peer relationships. Having a clearer picture of her likes and dislikes, she tends to base her friendships on mutual connection and common interests. Romantically, she may be heavily invested in an exclusive romantic relationship or she may be casually dating. Because she is at a stage where she is highly interested in dating and relationships, it is important that you speak with her about abstinence and sexual responsibility or refer her to places where she can go to get accurate information. Although middle adolescent females have stronger decision-making skills, it's still a good idea for you to guide them by stressing the importance of self-love, self-respect and self-responsibility as the foundation for healthy relationships with others.

Late Adolescence

During late adolescence all visible, physical, characteristics of childhood have disappeared. A little more growth in height and weight around the hips may occur as well as enlargement in breast size, but for the most part the late adolescent female has all the physical characteristics of a young woman.

Intellectually, she makes better decisions, begins to set long-term goals and is seriously concerned about her future. Throughout adolescence, African-American females struggle to find not only a personal identity but a cultural identity as well. This is heightened during late adolescence, because she begins to realize that no matter how she chooses to categorize or identify herself she is first and foremost a Black Female. And since she is influenced by two cultures, African and American, she must constantly look for ways to merge the two.

Emotionally, she is better able to manage her emotions. She learns that although adults tell her that it's ok to release her emotions, she will be taken more seriously, if she learns to control her emotional responses. This does not mean that she will not reach out for emotional support. It simply means that she will become more selective about whom she reaches out to and how she asks for help.

Morally, she has a clear sense of right and wrong and may even advocate and organize with others around her beliefs. She sees the social injustices of the world and often wants to do something to make a difference. She may join a student union, start an advocacy group or support a cause that she strongly believes in.

Socially, late adolescent females become increasingly aware that not only do they have to manage the normal adolescent tasks of preparing for independence; they have to develop life management skills for dealing with institutional racism and sexism. One of your tasks as a rites of passage leader is to help African-American young women develop coping and life management skills so that they can develop their full potential.

For African-American females, the journey to and through adolescence is not an easy one. Given the typical family structure of a female-headed household, additional responsibilities are often placed on the African-American female. Much of this is due to financial constraints within the family, the impact of oppression and limited resources. And as such African-American females bring a unique experience to the overall adolescent developmental process. What is needed to promote healthy adolescent female development in the context of the African-centered rites of passage program, is a solid understanding of the cultural orientation that African-American females bring to the process as well as how social factors such as; racism, sexism, and poverty impact on their development.

Connecting With African-American Girls and Young Women

In order to connect with African-American teenage girls and young women we must realize three things: First, our frame of reference is not their frame of reference, but this does not mean that we cannot bridge generational gaps. Second our heroes and sheroes are not necessarily theirs, but this does not mean that we cannot help them to understand how our heroes and sheroes paved the way for their heroes and sheroes. Third, our struggles are not entirely the same as theirs, but this does not mean that we cannot come together and make their struggles our struggles and our struggles their struggles.

1. Our frame of reference is not their frame of reference.

The generation that you were born into influences how you view, experience and engage in the world. For example, if you are an African-American of the 1950's generation, you would have probably listened to rock and roll music, had parents that did domestic work or hard manual labor, ate meals at the table with your family, and if you lived in the South you probably had to ride in the back of the bus. This would be your frame of reference along with the values that were predominant at that time. This frame of reference probably shapes most of what you say and do.

If you are a member of the late 1960's early 1970's generation and grew up during the Black Power/Black Pride movement you probably wore an Afro and Dashiki and were involved in improving the conditions of the Black Community. You would remember leaders such as Hewy Newton. You may be familiar with the Last Poets. You probably remember movies such as "Super Fly" and "Cleopatra Jones" some of your musical icons might be Marvin Gaye, Curtis Mayfield, Isaac Hayes and Aretha Franklin. This would be your frame of reference along with the values that were predominant at that time.

If you are a member of the old school hip hop generation (late 1970's early 1980's) you probably can recall the street jams in the parks. I would imagine that you could vividly remember the fashions, dances, language and predominant values of that time. You might have been the first one in your family to get an advanced degree or to own your own business. But you are also the first generation to feel the devastation of AIDS, Crack, and organized gang violence.

For the generation of youth who were largely impacted by Crack, AIDS, and absentee fathers and who were indoctrinated by M.T.V and B.E.T, where the values of materialism, sexual promiscuity, violence, and individualism are perpetuated; their frame of reference is somewhat different than the generations who came before them. As a result they are dealing with issues such as: guns in schools, easy access to drugs, profanity and explicit violence in music and movies, government interference in family child rearing practices, that previous generations did not have to contend with. This is why it is important that adults understand how one's generation impacts his/her frame of reference. The more we are able to understand this, the better we will be able to connect with youth, and bridge generational gaps.

2. Our heroes and sheroes are not necessarily theirs.

One year during Black History month I was invited to conduct a workshop on Black Sheroes for a girls mentoring program. I prepared an in-depth program that chronicled the lives of various African-American female achievers. As I began to discuss the contributions that women like Harriet Tubman, Rosa Parks, Toni Morrison, Susan Taylor, and Angela Davis made, somehow Mary J. Blige, Foxy Brown and Lil' Kim became the topic of discussion.

While I could see how Mary J. Blige was a sheroe because of her ability to overcome adversity and speak to women's issues through her music, I could not even begin to fathom how Lil' Kim could be held with such high regard, much less placed in the same category as my great sheroes. And while both of these women have achieved financial success, monetary achievement was not what "I" wanted to talk about. I wanted to talk about freedom fighters, civil rights activists, literary geniuses, feminists and social activists. But that was not what this group wanted to talk about, so I had to put my agenda aside and listen.

I started to ask the group questions about Mary J. Blige and Lil' Kim – specifically, what were the qualities and characteristics that made these women their sheroes? How did they challenge others to follow their dreams and become better people? Their responses about Mary J. Blige were very enlightening: "Mary keeps it real," " I can feel Mary's pain and she can feel mine." "Mary's a strong Black Woman," "In her music she talks about what I've been through or what I'm going through." Their responses about Lil' Kim were even more enlightening: "Lil' Kim goes after wants and makes it happen," "She doesn't care what other people think," "She doesn't let guys use her like all these other girls, she's in control of her sexuality," "Lil' Kim is in your face, like it or not." Their responses gave me a window into their world, their perceptions and their feelings, which forced me to ask another question: How could I get these young women to see that many of the internal qualities that they admired in Mary J. Blige and Lil' Kim were present in the sheroes of previous generations?

So the topic of the workshop became, "What makes a sheroe?' Some of their responses were: "A woman who stands up for what she believes in," "A female who is honest, fair and not only looks out for herself but reaches back to help others," "A female who is able to stand strong even during difficult times," "A female who doesn't let what other people say and do make or break her," "A female who does what she has to do to survive and make a better way for her children," "A female who knows what she wants and doesn't let anything stop her."

As each girl gave her response, I helped the group to draw correlations between the women who they admired and the female achievers who came before them. The results were pretty amazing. Together we were able to connect the past to the present, the young to the old, the flamboyant to the subdued as a result they were able to realize that we all need each other to survive, succeed and create a better future – that without a Madame C.J. Walker there wouldn't be a Mary J. Blige or without a Harriet Tubman there wouldn't be a Queen Latifah.

One of the first principles that I learned in my social work training was to meet the client where the client was at. This principle makes good sense. When you meet young women where they are mentally, emotionally and socially, you will be better able to reach them.

3. Our struggles are not entirely the same as their struggles.

Each generation has its' own unique set of struggles. For many African-Americans who are members of the 1950's and 60's generation, the causes they championed had to do with civil rights and women's rights, the right to vote, the right to equal education, the right to eat where they wanted and the right to equal pay for equal labor. For African-American of the 1970's generation their struggles were about building Black pride, building social programs that were for and run by Blacks and fighting for social justice. For African-Americans of the 1980's generation their struggles were about brining attention to issues that impacted their quality of life and their communities.

For many generation X African-Americans their struggle is about survival and finding hope in a society that seems to have given up on them. If you listen to the music and movies of today's popular youth culture, you will be able to better understand the struggles that young people are faced with. In a record entitled "Everyday Struggle" by the late rapper Notorious B.I.G. the chorus goes

"I don't wanna live no more sometime I see death knockin at my front door." This record reveals an aspect of youth culture that many adults do not know how to deal with: despair, isolation, hopelessness and survival by any means necessary.

As we begin to listen to youth, specifically young women, with a willing heart and an open mind we will get a clearer picture of the issues that impact their lives. As a result, we will be better able to bridge generational gaps and help them develop the skills and resources that they need to become strong, emotionally healthy, high achieving young women.

4

African-American Young Females and Their Relationships

African-American culture is built on a foundation of kinship and community that goes back to our traditional, communal way of life in Africa. In other words, African-Americans are a people who believe in community. By nature of our cultural principles and practices, many of us connect with and relate to one another in a familial way. This is why many African-Americans still adhere to the old African proverb, "it takes a village to raise one child."

If you are to help African-American teenage girls and young women build healthier relationships with themselves and others, you need to look at their relationship imprinting (the messages they received growing up about love, intimacy, womanhood and Black males.) Further, you need to identify behaviors that indicate the internalization of negative myths and messages concerning African-American relationships.

It's important to remember that there was a time when African-American families were intact. Research indicates that before the 1960's, the African-American family was a stable unit that provided support, cohesion and connection not only among biological members, but among non-related African-American as well. During and after slavery when families were split up; African-Americans established associations to help them re-establish family bonds and expand their circle of support. Historically, African-Americans have understood the importance of building a supportive family network, whether biological or chosen.

Despite the proud history and desire to build and maintain strong communities, there is a relationship crisis in the African-American community, and our youth are gravely affected by it. From the continual breakdown of the Black family, to the growing distrust and hostility between African-American males and females, to the increased backbiting and belittling that occurs between women, these issues impact on the young women whom you are working with. Helping females build healthier relationships isn't just about getting them to respect themselves and understand the difference between nurturing, supportive relationships and emotionally draining ones, it's also about understanding: the special dynamics that occur between African-American mothers and daughters, the impact that an absent father has on a female's ability to trust males, the importance of developing healthy female friendships in order to expand one's circle of support and how healthy love begins with self-love.

The Special Dynamics Between African-American Mothers and Daughters

The relationship between an African-American mother and her daughter often comes with many challenges and special dynamics. For the African-American mother not only is she raising her daughter, she is also modeling what it means to be female even if she's not consciously aware of it. No matter how hard a mother tries not to over-identify with her daughter, she can't help but see herself all over again as she raises her daughter and this adds a special dimension to the African-American mother/daughter relationship.

While a mother nurtures and protects her son and often allows him to "get away" with more than her daughter, for her daughter she models what she believes to be appropriate behavior and she instills a sense of responsibility that is different from how she raises her son. This can affect a daughter in profound ways. She often grows up believing that she is less worthy, lovable and deserving than a male and without realizing it she often repeats the same pattern when she becomes a mother. Hence we coin the expression that, "Black mothers love their sons, but raise their daughters."

There is a long and painful history that has brought about this difference in the way that African-American mothers raise their sons. During and after slavery, Black males were hung, castrated and beaten beyond recognition in order to keep them in their "place" and to breed fear and division among the African-American people. Although African-Americans are not physically enslaved, many African-American mothers still feel the psychological impact of slavery, particularly when it comes to raising their boys. But today instead of Black boys being lynched with rope, they are beaten with clubs or brutally gunned down by police. Historically, for the African-American female, the worst that could happen was that she would be raped. And while rape is a traumatic and painful experience, mothers knew based on their own experiences and the experiences of their foremothers that their daughters could survive a rape. But their sons could not survive a lynching.

The fear among African-American mothers of the targeted and calculated death of their sons is still as real and present today, as it was in the past. All we have to do is recall the numerous incidents of African-American males who were brutally beaten and killed by police to see that the fear of death for black males is still as real today as it was in the past. It is this fear coupled with the socialization process that causes many African-American mothers to give special consideration to the care of their sons. And sometimes this special care breeds resentment in their daughters.

How does the special consideration of sons affect African-American daughters? On one hand they may become overachievers in order to gain the approval and affection of their mothers, but on the other hand they may grow to resent the differential treatment that their mothers showed toward the male children and as a result they may either rebel or withdraw. When a daughter receives the message either implicitly or explicitly that she is less lovable than the male children, she may internalize these feelings and behave in ways that reinforce her negative feelings. For example, she may not perform up to her full potential, she may direct her anger towards her brother or other males, or she may engage in self-destructive behaviors in an attempt to get the love and attention that she did not receive at home.

Based on the mother's experiences and upbringing, she often believes that it is necessary to encourage maturity and responsibility in her daughter at a young age. If the mother was left to raise her children alone, she may believe that men cannot be trusted or counted on for support and may subconsciously pass down these beliefs to her daughter. As a result she often expects her daughter to take on the majority of the household responsibilities even if there are male children living in the home. It is in the arena of the home that African-American mothers teach their daughters about becoming a woman, because this is where they spend the most time together.

Girls are always taking in messages from their mothers. And whether or not the daughter is aware of it, she takes her cues about her self-worth, womanhood and how to be in the world from her mother. The messages that a mother sends both consciously and subconsciously are taken in by her daughter and affects how she understands the world and her role in society. A mother's every word and action is a message for her daughter about: how to live, what to do, what not to do, what's expected of her and how she is loved. Depending on the mother's own upbringing, level of self-worth, values, expectations, unrealized dreams and feelings toward her mother, she will either indicate acceptance of her daughter or rejection.

One way to understand the dynamic between African-American mothers and daughters is to examine the "code of being," that is passed down from mother to daughter. A code of being can be defined as rules and strong convictions passed down from parent or caretaker to child about how one "should be" and "ought to live." A code of being is very powerful because it is passed down without question from one generation to the next. Usually, a code of being is not open for discussion or negotiation, because it is considered to be the truth and it is the foundation for survival in that particular home. For example, a common code of being for many African-American females is to be totally self-reliant and independent. While self-reliance and independence are necessary characteristics for successful independent living, the problem comes in when these characteristics prevent one from asking for or accepting help.

What can you do to help adolescent females develop healthier relationships with their mothers?

- **Encourage open communication.**
  Open communication is an important ingredient in helping daughters develop healthier relationships with their mothers. Encourage the young women you are working with to talk to their

mothers about issues that are important to them. Although adolescent females are at a time in their lives where they are spending more time with peers, they should still be encouraged to spend time with their families and talk to their parents about important life issues.

- **Help mothers to support their daughter's through this developmental stage.**
  Mothers need to understand what typical adolescent female development looks like and how to support their daughters through this process. Mothers also need to understand that they play a critical role in the development of their daughter's self-esteem and should be encouraged to give positive praise, nurture their daughter's talents as well as help them set goals.

- **Help initiates identify mother figures.**
  There will be girls and young women in your program who have severely strained or severed relationships with their mothers and as a result will need to identify mother figures in order to get some of their mothering needs met. Even girls who have close relationships with their mothers can benefit by having a mentor or "adopted mother" because they will not tell their mothers everything that is going on in their lives no matter how much their mothers insist that they will.

- **Encourage mothers to become involved in your rites of passage program.**
  When mothers become involved in the rites of passage program, they demonstrate support for their daughters and they model the principle of community involvement. You can enlist the mothers' involvement by asking them to teach a class, chaperone a trip or volunteer where needed. It is important however, that you do not allow mothers to facilitate or take part in the group rap sessions because this may prevent initiates from speaking openly. The only exception is if you hold a special rap session for mothers and daughters.

It is wonderful when adolescent girls have close, supportive relationships with their mothers. But unfortunately this will not always be the case. Some girls may have severely strained relationships with their mothers or they may have severed ties all together. If this is the case, then you may want to think about bringing in a trained professional to help them begin to work through these issues. For girls who live with foster families or in congregate care settings, you may find that the mother/daughter relationship is a sensitive subject and you may even notice that some of the girls have unresolved hostility towards their mothers. You will need to address these issues carefully and sensitively as they arise. And if you are struggling with your own unresolved issues towards your mother, some of the experiences that initiates share, may bring up strong feelings for you. Make sure to do your own healing work beforehand, if you suspect that you might be harboring any unresolved issues towards your mother.

Following is a ceremony that you can perform to help the young women you are working with forgive their mothers' real and perceived transgressions. Forgiveness is an important part of the growth process. It allows us to make peace with our past, move forward and stop painful experiences (real or perceived) from preventing us from reaching our full potential. This ceremony is recommended for young women seventeen years of age and older. There is no recommended time for this ceremony. You should use your professional judgment to decide on the appropriate time in your program for this ceremony. And when you feel led to carry out this ceremony, make sure that you have dealt with your own issues regarding your mother. Also, be sure that group cohesion has taken place.

Forgiving Mother

The tools you will need for this ceremony are:

- Lavender incense for peace and healing
- Myrrh incense for new beginnings and purification
- Vanilla candle for light, love and warmth
- A journal for each initiate
- Soft music playing in the background (optional)

Begin the process of forgiveness and healing by standing or sitting in a circle and saying aloud: "I seek to release all the negative feelings that I have towards my mother in order to move forward and allow healing to take place." Light the myrrh incense and place it in the middle of the circle. Then light the lavender incense place it in the middle of the circle and say, "I seek to forgive the woman who delivered me into this world and I accept that she loved me the best way that she knew how." Give each participant a vanilla candle and starting with yourself direct participants to light the candle of the person on their left until all of the candles have been lit. Raising your candles in front of you say, " I welcome light, love and warmth into my life." "I am loved." "I am whole." "I am destined for great things." "My past does not determine my future." I have the power to take charge of my future." Then blow out the candles. Starting with yourself, have each participant place her candle in the center of the circle.

Distribute the journals and have each initiate answer these questions:

1. If I could tell my mother anything in the world about what angers me most about her, what would I say?
2. How do I think my mom would respond to what I have to say?
3. What are the possible reasons why my mother was not able to meet my needs in the way that I needed her to meet them? Did she have a drug or alcohol problem? Anger towards my father that she took out on me? Unresolved relationship issues with her own mother? An abusive past? Is she mentally ill or emotionally unstable?
4. What steps can I take to let go of the anger that I have towards my mother so that I am no longer controlled by my negative feelings toward her?

When initiates are finished, have them share their journal entries with the group and encourage group members to offer non-judgmental, supportive, feedback. Afterward, you should offer each initiate feedback regarding what she can do to start the healing and forgiveness process. Remember, you are dealing with a sensitive subject and strong feelings may emerge. Be sure that ceremony leaders have solid counseling skills so that they can address any issues that may arise.

You can end the ceremony with affirmations such as: "I am loved." "I am strong." "I am good." "I am beautiful." Or you can end the ceremony with a guided meditation or non-denominational prayer.

African-American Girls and Their Fathers

The relationship that a girl has with her father will impact the relationships that she has with other males. When a girl has a close, healthy relationship with her father, it strengthens her self-confidence and gives her a solid foundation upon which to build other relationships with males on. But when a girl grows up without her father, or has an unhealthy relationship with him, she misses out on the paternal support and nurturing that is necessary for healthy growth and development to take place.

A girl's father represents her first image of manhood. He provides her with a context for understanding the paternal role that a man plays in his family. When a girl has a negative image of her father, she often carries this mental picture in her heart and mind and it affects how she views and relates to other males. For example, if a girl was abandoned, rejected or abused by her father she is likely to carry these feelings over into her relationships with other males. As a result she grow up expecting the absolute worst from men.

When I conduct workshops for young women on, how to build healthy relationships with males, I ask them to describe the relationships that they have with their fathers. The responses that I get most often are, "I don't have a relationship with my father." "I never met my father." "My mother is my father." "I see my father from time to time, because he has another family." Their responses indicate that far too many relationships between African-American daughters and their fathers are either strained, superficial, or non-existent. This is not to say that there aren't wonderful African-American fathers who are active in their children's lives, but we cannot deny that the absence of fathers is a crisis in the African-American community.

Although many women have successfully raised their children, for the purposes of this book, their daughters, single-handedly, children still need their fathers. Growing up without a father can impact a girl's development in a number of ways. If a girl has unresolved abandonment issues with her father, she may look for paternal love by engaging in sexual relationships with much older males. If a girl was abused by her father, she may unconsciously end up in relationships where the abusive patterns are repeated – thus the negative feelings that she carries about herself and males are reinforced.

What can you do to help females develop healthier relationships with their fathers, and when that is not possible how can you help them get their paternal needs met in appropriate ways?

Encourage your girls to talk about their fathers.

It is important that you encourage the girls and young women in your program to talk about their fathers. They can share as much or as little as they feel comfortable sharing. The key is to get them talking about the kinds of relationships they have with their fathers.

Encourage fathers to play an active role in their daughters' lives.

When a father plays an active role in his daughter's life, he demonstrates support, protection and security. Even if the father is not living in the home, he can play an active role by getting involved in his daughter's education and the various other programs that she is participating in. He can advise her on important issues and give her ongoing emotional support. Through casual conversations with fathers you can discuss the important role that they play in their daughter's growth and development.

Encourage fathers to play a process-oriented role in their daughters' lives when they cannot play a structured role

When a father cannot or will not play an active role in his daughter's life, encourage him to play a process-oriented role. A process-oriented role has to do with contributing to the development of values, beliefs, and internal codes of conduct regarding his daughter's interactions with males, position on sex and her decisions regarding relationships. When a father's role is process-oriented his function, by example and candid discussion is to provide his daughter with insight into African-American males and how to appropriately relate to them. A father's function in a process-oriented role is to inform his daughter of the social, political and economic conditions that impact the African-American male, how he views himself and African-American females, how to set appropriate boundaries with males, and how to establish healthy, nurturing relationships with males. When a father's role is process-oriented, he will positively contribute to how his daughter sees herself and other males. Even if a father is in prison he can play a process-oriented role in his daughter's life, through letter writing, telephone calls and when she goes to visit him.

Encourage fathers to become involved in some aspect of your rites of passage program.

Whether it is leading a one-time group on male/female relationships or leading a special sports activity, it is important that initiates have access to positive, male role models. You can also coordinate a special event such as a father/daughter day.

Help initiates build healthy relationships with positive adult male role models.

When relationships with fathers are severely strained or nonexistent, it may not be possible to help the young women in your program develop healthy relationships with their fathers. However, it is still important that they find healthy ways to get their paternal needs met. One way that you can facilitate this process is by encouraging initiates to develop non-sexual relationships with adult males. Male role models can provide paternal nurturing, support, guidance and serve in the role of extended family member, or "adopted father." It is important that you get permission and support from the initiates' mothers so that they are aware and in agreement with what you are trying to accomplish. If a girl already has a close, non-sexual relationship with an adult male, find out who he is and ask if you and her mother could meet him. This is important, because it enables you to find out if his intentions are honorable and it allows you and the mothers to set appropriate boundaries. Once you identify a male who will serve as a role model or adopted father, it is important that you and the initiate discuss the role that he will play in her life and that you set some boundaries for both the initiate and the male role model.

I am now going to guide you through a ritual that is designed to help young women release any negative feelings that they may have towards their fathers. By releasing the negative feelings that they have towards their fathers they can begin to move forward. This ritual is recommended for young women seventeen years of age and older. Just as you did with the "forgiving mother" ritual make sure that you have dealt with your own issues concerning your father. Also, make sure that group cohesion has taken place and that skilled counselors are on hand.

Making Peace With My Father

The tools that you will need for this ritual are:

- A plastic bowl filled with water for each participant.
- A white flower for each participant (represents nature's gift of beauty, purity and innocence)
- Sandalwood incense for healing (have it lit in the background before the ceremony begins)

Begin by having initiates sit in a circle. Then, give each initiate a bowl of water and ask her to place it by her feet. Ask initiates to close their eyes and imagine that it's four years from now. They are successful college students or starting a career that they really enjoy. It's Saturday afternoon and they have just received a letter from a close friend. This is a friend who has been there for them through thick and thin. This is someone who they completely trust.

This close friend discloses that she is angry with her father, but never had the opportunity to tell him. She feels hurt, abandoned and betrayed, and she doesn't want to feel this way anymore. This close friend asks each person's advice on how to deal with her anger so that she can make peace with her past. She goes around the room and asks each initiate to share one piece of advice or some words of encouragement to help her cope. Ask each initiate to suggest a healthy way that the close friend can begin to heal the anger that she is carrying toward her father.

Ask each initiate to get a picture in her mind of this close friend. Tell them to study her face very carefully. Inform them that as they look at her more closely, they notice that the close friend is them (it is their wise inner-self who they can call on for wisdom and direction). Tell each initiate to call upon her wise inner-self to find the strength and resilience to release any negative feelings that she has towards her father. Direct initiates to pick up their bowls and release any negative feelings that they have about themselves or their fathers into the water. When they are finished have them get up one-by-one, pour the water out, toss the bowls into a trash can and go back to their seats.

Next, give each girl a flower; instruct her to hold it next to her heart. Then you say: "These flowers represent your beauty, purity and all that is good in you." "Keep this flower as a memento to represent the healing and forgiveness that is blossoming in your hear." "Whenever you begin to feel hurt, betrayed or abandoned by your father, take out your flower to remind yourself of your commitment to releasing the negative feelings that you have towards him so that you don't become overwhelmed or defeated by anger."

Next, ask each girl to say aloud: "I am lovable, worthy and whole." " I will not let negative feelings defeat me." " I replace all negativity in my life with peace." These affirmations will set into motion an empowered attitude that will enable healing to begin. Africans call the power of spoken declaration or affirmation Afose, which means the power to bring about occurrence by way of speech.

Female Friendships

Traditionally, African-American females both young and old viewed each other as family, not as competition for males, jobs, or resources. Traditionally, African-American females understood that they survived and excelled by, through and with each other – that is why they often refer to one another as sister. In West African Ashanti culture, cultural life and the communal bond was shaped and preserved by women. In the Ashanti culture the queen mother (Ohemaa) served as the senior female of the tribe who guided the other women by overseeing female rites of passage activities and initiation ceremonies, as well as acting as the official genealogist so that women could trace their ancestral lineage.

Females of African ancestry have a history of supporting each other. Traditionally, African-American women have relied on communal support from the sisterhood to assist with child rearing, taking care of the home, emotional support, mentoring and helping the younger women prepare themselves for adulthood. African-American females knew that if they wanted to create a network where they could be themselves, shed their daily burdens, and create a better life for themselves as well as the next generation they had to stick together.

A supportive female network is key to a young woman's healthy growth and development. Not only does it enlarge her circle of support, but it also provides a healthy foundation upon which to build relationships with males on. In my work and personal experience with African American teenage girls and young women I have found that many of them do not trust other females. When I asked them to tell me why, the most common responses were: "I was taught not to trust females, because if you let them get too close they will stab you in the back." "My mother told me to be leery of other females, especially around my man." "I used to be real cool with this girl at school, but then I found out she was talking about me behind my back – females are trifling."

As you can see, based on the messages that they received or personal experiences some African American girls have negative beliefs about other females. As a rites of passage facilitator, it is important that you help initiates to develop more positive attitudes about other females and build healthier female friendships. One way to facilitate this process is by helping initiates to preserve the traditions and attitudes that African-American females have traditionally practiced such as: thinking of each other as sisters, offering support and guidance, respecting the sister's relationship code of conduct by leaving each other's boyfriends alone, and getting to know and respect other females before deciding that they do not like or trust them.

Another way to help initiates build stronger relationships with other girls is to help them recognize the small ways that girls and young women show each other that they are sisters such as: offering words of encouragement during a difficult time, listening without judgment while another female shares something that is important to her, doing a kind deed for another female without expecting anything in return, or any other behavior that demonstrates love, caring, kindness, support, understanding and friendship.

There is a growing hunger for sisterhood among African–American women. This is why so many sister-friend groups are being formed. When we teach girls and young women to get to know, respect and appreciate each other we help them to build relationships that can strengthen, enhance and enrich their lives. A girl's choice to dislike another female needs to be as clear as her choice to initiate a friendship. When girls dislike each other before getting to know one another they limit their support system.

Developing healthy female friendships happens one step at a time and it requires trust and commitment. However challenging it may be, it is an important part of a young woman's growth and development. The rites of passage experience in itself fosters an environment of sisterhood. With your guidance and by your example, you can help initiates develop an unbreakable bond with one another that they will carry in their hearts and minds for the rest of their lives.

Her Relationships With African-American Males

It is part of the natural developmental process for adolescent females to develop close friendships and romantic relationships with males. Whether a young woman wants to casually date or have an exclusive romantic relationship, it is important that she knows how to identify the characteristics of a healthy relationship. Equipped with this information she will be better able to make dating and relationship choices that protect her best interests and respect her boundaries. As African-American young women begin to date, they will experience the ups and downs of male/female relationships. And whether they realize it or not, they will bring the relationship lessons that they've learned through family experiences into their male/female relationships. The males will also bring the lessons that they learned about manhood, females and relationships into their male/female relationships. And when the two come together, they must seek to understand themselves and each other in order to build and sustain healthy relationships.

In order for this to happen African-American males and females must learn to trust, honor and respect each other; which starts by trusting, honoring and respecting one's self. Although you probably will not be working honoring and respecting one's self. Although you probably will not be working with males, you can provide the young women whom you are working with the tools and information that they can use to develop healthier relationships with males. This will enable initiates to make healthier dating and relationship choices.

Much can be said about the state of relationships between young African-American males and females. Some are characterized by mutual trust, respect and admiration, but many are characterized by mistrust, blatant disrespect, a get-all-you-can attitude, or a disposable mentality. Unfortunately, many of the values and attitudes that young males and females bring to their relationships are a reflection of what they see and hear in the media, their homes, their communities, and in the larger society.

African-American young women live in a very different world than their foremothers. Traditionally, African-American women were honored and in many ways considered to be the backbone of not only their families, but the Black community as well. Before the 1970's, relationships between African-American males and females were tightly bonded on the basis of shared experiences, traditional values and mutual respect. And together they were a unified force. Historically in the African-American community, trust and mutual respect were the cornerstones of the community and enabled Black men and Black women to build secure bonds, strong families and tightly-knit communities.

But in today's world much of that has changed. With the birth of gangsta rap, a genre of rap music that grew popular in the mid 1980's and reflects the harsh realities of life on the streets, African-American females went from being highly revered to blatantly disrespected. As a member of the first generation of old school hip-hop, I have seen hip-hop's evolution and witnessed how the values and attitudes reflected in gangsta rap have affected the psyche of youth and the state of African-American, male/female relationships.

African-American females receive the most sexist and disrespectful attacks from gangsta rap and sometimes the hip-hop community at large. In rap music, and in hip-hop videos females are often exploited and reduced to mere body parts. In gangsta rap women are almost never referred to as queens or ladies like they used to be in old school rap. Instead we've become skeezers, hood rats, chicken heads, baby's momma's and at worst bitches and hoes. We've been reduced from the backbone of the family and the African-American community to headless poultry *(chicken heads)*, female dogs *(bitches)*, neighborhood rodents *(hood rats)*, and inanimate sex objects *(T & A Eye Candy)*.

What is also very disturbing is that many young females specifically, African-American have internalized these messages and images so deeply that they've become de-sensitized and in some respects accepting of the sexism and blatant disrespect. Many have also bought into the value of materialism and as a result have adopted the "no romance without finance" mindset. Many young women use the promise of sex as a trump card to gain status, material possessions, and power. And the sad thing is they do not realize that they are disrespecting themselves in the process.

What does this mean for you as a rites of passage facilitator as you set out to assist African-American females in developing healthy relationships with males?

It means that you need to help young women examine their attitudes about themselves, males and the status of male/female relationships. It also means that you need to help young women: get clear about their values, develop standards of acceptable behavior, set appropriate boundaries, and understand the difference between a healthy and an unhealthy relationship.

Following are some tips that will enable you to help African-American young women build healthier relationships with males.

- **Help young women identify unhealthy relationship practices.**

Stress that a healthy relationship is built on mutual respect and trust, not drama and pain. If initiates are behaving in ways that are hurtful, harmful or self-destructive bring the behavior to their attention and openly discuss your reasons for concern. If they are accepting behavior that is hurtful and demeaning help them to see how putting up with the behavior causes them more harm than good.

- **Help young women to set acceptable standards of behavior.**

Help young women to develop internal guidelines for themselves and to be clear about what these values are. Stress the importance of respect, treating one's body like a temple and not accepting abusive or disrespectful behavior.

- **Help young women to assess their level of relationship readiness.**

No matter how old you are, building and sustaining a healthy relationship takes work. More importantly, one should be ready before one engages in a relationship. It is important to help a young woman assess whether or not she is ready to engage in an exclusive romantic relationship, if she should casually date or if she should hold off on dating all together. In order to have a healthy relationship with someone else, one needs to be clear about one's values, have good decision making skills and have a healthy relationship with oneself. If a young woman does not have a healthy relationship with herself as well as clearly defined values, then she is not ready for a relationship with someone else.

- **Help young women to assert themselves.**

Sometimes in order to fit in with the crowd and gain the approval of her peers, a young woman may engage in behaviors that go against what she truly believes. Help young women to develop assertiveness skills and peer pressure refusal skills so that they can be true to themselves.

- **Help young women to understand the consequences of engaging in a sexual relationship prematurely.**

It is very important that young women understand the consequences of engaging in a sexual relationship prematurely like: an unplanned pregnancy, a sexually transmitted disease, a scarred reputation, a diminished sense of self-worth, or the relationship not working out as they hoped. This is why it is so important that you stress to your young women that they should treat their bodies like temples, and decide what their position will be on sex before they get caught up in the heat of the moment.

- **Help young women understand the difference between sex and intimacy.**

Sex is a physical act while intimacy is a spiritual, emotional, and intellectual connection that enables both people to share their innermost thoughts and feelings. Sexual chemistry is based on physical attraction, while an intimate connection is based on trust, safety, respect, validation, and mutual sharing. Because of the socialization process, many young women have difficulty differentiating between sex and intimacy. They often believe that having sex with a guy will make the guy love them, stay with them or bring the two of them closer. And oftentimes after the fact, they regret that they engaged in sex prematurely. This is why it is important that young women are encouraged to develop intimate relationships with males rather than sexual ones.

- **Help young women to show off their best feature – their minds.**

Popular music, movies and magazines try to make young women believe that they have to behave promiscuously or dress provocatively to attract guys. While this may be the case in the fantasy world of media, this is not the case for the average young African-American female. It is important to teach young women that they have much more to offer than their bodies. By placing the focus on the mind rather than the body, you teach young women to approach relationships with male peers from an empowered and self-respecting position.

- **Help young women separate facts from popular stereotypes.**

"All males are dogs." "All females are materialistic." These are negative stereotypes that are often perpetuated in the African-American community. Help young women not to buy into the negative myths and stereotypes concerning African-American males. Provide young women with positive examples that counteract the negative messages that they receive.

- **Help young women to decipher the messages that they receive from the media about themselves and males.**

Sit down with young women and find out about the messages they receive from popular music, movies and magazines. Use this as an opportunity to start a dialogue about male/female relationship issues.

- **Help young women learn how to love, value and respect themselves**

As you already know a healthy relationships with someone else begins with a healthy relationship with self. Help young women to realize that until they love, care for, respect and value themselves, they will not be able to develop a healthy relationship with anyone else. Real love cannot exist without knowledge and love of self. The more a young woman knows and loves herself, the better able she will be to build a healthy relationship with someone else.

5

Getting Started:
Preliminary Preparations for A Successful Program

As with any new program, preparation is key to your success. The clearer you are about what you want to do and how you intend to do it, the greater your chances of delivering a successful rites of passage program. With many new programs, most people use the hit-or-miss approach. Meaning, they offer a new program without thinking through all of the pertinent details such as: the needs of the target population, making sure the program fits with the overall mission and vision of the host organization and mapping out a plan to crystallize the concept. If the program is successful, then it's a hit. But if it is not, then it's a miss and everyone suffers, especially the people who your program was intended to serve. You can avoid the pitfalls of the hit-or-miss approach, if you do your planning in advance (before you actually carry out your rites program). Before you begin to share your program ideas with others, before you talk to prospective initiates, you should think about your overall goal, your objectives, how much you think the program will cost and the methods that you will use to measure and monitor progress. By thinking through all of the details in advance, you increase your chances of creating a successful program.

Conducting A Needs Assessment

Why conduct a needs assessment? For two reasons: First, to help determine whether or not there is a need for a rites of passage program in your community or organization. Second, to develop the program content. Conducting a needs assessment makes good sense. It allows you to find out if the rites of passage program that you want to offer is consistent with your organization's mission. And this information will better enable you to get organizational support in terms of money and resources. Second, it allows you to find out what services are already being offered in your community or organization so that you do not duplicate services and if you do, you'll be able to offer a higher level of programming because you'll know what's working and what's not. Without an assessment, it will be difficult to run a successful rites program, because you will not have the necessary background information to competently meet the needs of your target population. Further, the information acquired from the needs assessment can be a useful sales tool to sell the program to colleagues, upper management and sponsors. Further, a needs assessment can be a useful tool to gain funding for your program.

Here are some examples of how needs assessments can be conducted.

1. **Questionnaires** – can be in the form of surveys or polls. You can use a variety of questioning formats such as: open-ended, priority-ranking, fill-ins and multiple-choice.
2. **Published Works** – can be in the form of a case study, a report from a sample group, professional articles and trade journals. Recently published works provide current, cutting-edge information.
3. **Focus Groups** – can be formal or informal and may be used with a variety of groups such as: youth, line staff, administrative staff, board members or samples from each group.
4. **Organizational Records** – may consist of staff reports, program records, group meeting notes and internal program studies.
5. **Consulting with Professionals In The Field** – is a good way to find out about current trends problems and issues.

Developing Goals and Objectives

Once you've conducted a needs assessment, you are ready to develop goals and objectives. A clear sense of where you want to go and what you want to accomplish are the most important elements in designing a successful program. If you are not clear about your goals and objectives, you may overlook some of the important factors that will aid in the success of your program. Further, clearly defined goals and objectives provide those who are involved in your program with a sense of purpose, direction and accountability.

In this section I have provided you with suggested goals and objectives for an African-centered, female rites of passage program. The suggested goals and objectives are presented to serve as a guide. However, as you reflect on the needs of your intended female population as well as your host organization, you may find that you need to make some adjustments in your goals and objectives. In order to stay in line with your organization's mission, you may need to make alterations and adaptations. But no matter what changes you implement, keep in mind that in order to keep the program authentic, you need to stay true to the cultural integrity of the program.

Overall Program Goal

The overall goal of an African-centered female rites of passage program is to provide girls and young women of African heritage with the skills, knowledge and habits that will enable them to prepare themselves culturally, spiritually, mentally, physically and emotionally for the successful passage into womanhood.

Once you have stated the overall program goal, the next step is to establish learning goals, for the initiates. There are three types of learning goals: affective, cognitive and behavioral.

1. Affective learning goals

Affective learning goals focus on the formation of attitudes, beliefs and feelings. In the context of an African-centered female rites of passage program some of the affective learning goals that you may want to establish for initiates are:

- To explore their feelings regarding their African heritage;
- To explore their beliefs and attitudes about womanhood;
- To examine to what extent that the messages they receive from their families and the media impact their self-concept.

2. Cognitive learning goals

Cognitive learning goals focus on acquiring new information and concepts. In the context of an African-centered female rites of passage program, some of the cognitive learning goals that you may want to establish for the initiates are:

- To identify the seven principles of Nguzo Saba and apply them to their daily lives;
- To identify the seven virtues of MAAT and describe how they can apply them to their interpersonal relationships;
- To describe the benefits of incorporating African-centered principles into their lives.

3. Behavioral learning goals

Behavioral learning goals focus on learning new behavior and developing competency in a specific area. In the context of an African-centered female rites of passage program some of the behavioral goals that you may want to establish are:

- Initiates attending a workshop on assertiveness are provided with hypothetical situations and practice how to set boundaries and stand up for themselves;
- Initiates learn how to write down their personal, educational, and career goals in a step-by-step fashion;
- Initiates learn and practice peer pressure refusal sills to effectively handle negative peer pressure.

After you have outlined the learning goals for initiates, the next step is to establish objectives or outcomes. These should represent the concrete accomplishments that you want initiates to attain as a result of going through your rites of passage program. Following are some suggested objectives:

At the conclusion of the rights of passage program initiates will be better able to:

- Define and describe at least three factors that impact on the development of self-esteem in African-American females;
- Identify their values and describe how their personal values affect their day-to-day choices;
- Compare and contrast the characteristics of a healthy relationship with the characteristics of an unhealthy one;
- Use effective communication skills to articulate their needs and desires;
- Use conflict resolution skills to de-escalate conflicts with peers;
- Identify self-imposed barriers to healthy living and overcome resistance to change;
- Use creative self-expression as a vehicle for personal growth;
- Explain their new role in the development of their relationships, communities and society at large;
- Increase appropriate use of time, and money;
- Demonstrate an appreciation of traditional African and African-American culture;
- Practice self-nurturing and self-care rituals on a consistent basis;
- Identify self-defeating habits and avoid them;
- Develop a personal action plan in order to continue making positive choices.

Goals and Objectives Worksheet

Although I have provided suggested goals and objectives for you, it's a good idea to establish some of your own. Think about the female rites of passage program that you want to offer and write out your goals and objectives.

- Affective Learning Goals

_____

_____

_____

_____

_____

- Behavioral Learning Goals

_____

_____

_____

_____

_____

- Cognitive Learning Goals

_____

_____

_____

_____

_____

- Objectives

_____

_____

_____

_____

_____

_____

_____

_____

_____

_____

Drafting A Written Proposal

After you have conducted the needs assessment and established program goals and objectives, the next step is developing the written proposal. This outlines the specifics in terms of how you intend to implement the program. A written proposal will help you: sell the program idea to others, answer specific questions that administrators, volunteers, parents, initiates and other key people will want to know, and it is a tool that could aid you in getting your program funded. The proposal does not have to be long and drawn out, three to five pages should be sufficient.

In the written proposal you want to be sure to include: a statement of need, program description, goals and objectives, program design, program logistics and procedures, projected time-line, evaluation procedures and a proposed budget.

1. A statement of need
You've already conducted the needs assessment. Use it as the basis for your statement of need. A statement of need describes the problem or issue to be addressed and why your particular program is necessary.

2. Program description
A program description describes the essence of your program. It is a brief overview of your program. It is a brief overview of your program's vision and mission as well as how you intend to deliver the program.

3. Goals and objectives
Since you've already established program goals and objectives, all you have to do is transfer this information to this portion of the proposal. If you are developing your own objectives make sure that they are concrete and measurable. Also, make sure that they are reasonable for the age and abilities of the initiates as well as the length of the program.

4. Program design
The program design describes the layout of the program. In this section include the program components, activities and services you will offer such as: peer group rap sessions, field trips, community service projects, independent study projects, initiation retreat, crossover ceremony and any other activities and services that you wish to offer.

5. Program logistics and procedures
Program logistics and procedures addresses who will do what and how it will get done. Some questions that you need to consider in this area are:
* How many females will your program serve?
* What criteria will you use to select members? (age, geographical location, etc.)

- Where will the program meet?
- How often will initiates meet?
- How long will the program be? (twelve months, nine months, six months, three months)
- What will you do if initiates want to drop out?
- Who will coordinate the program?
- How will the program be staffed? (In-house staff, consultants, hiring new staff, volunteers)
- How will you recruit initiates and volunteers?
- How will you involve parents?
- Who will be responsible for program documentation?

These are just a few of the questions that you should consider for the aforementioned section.

6. Projected time-line
A projected time-line enables you to focus on your goals and chart the program's progress from start to finish. The time-line can be broken down monthly for nine to twelve month programs and weekly for six to three month programs. Be sure to include time for start-up and planning in your time-line. Start-up time allows time for recruitment, developing flyers and brochures, conducting additional research and identifying volunteers and sponsors.

7. Evaluation procedures
Evaluation procedures allow you to measure and monitor the program's progress and success. In the evaluation segment of the proposal you need to state: how you will determine if the program goals and objectives have been met, how you will obtain evaluative data about the initiates, and how you will evaluate staff performance. You should also include plans for follow-up.

8. Proposed budget
Whenever you are proposing a new initiative to a group or organization the question that is lingering in the back of their minds is, "How much is it going to cost?" You do not have to be a mathematical genius to put together a budget, all you have to do is a little research. Write down everything that you think you will need for your program, including: material, supplies, food, labor (unless your program will be staffed by volunteers) retreat site (such as a camp, dude ranch, or retreat center unless you will be utilizing someone's home or you have access to free space) plaques and certificates to be given out at the conclusion of the crossover ceremony, and anything else that you think you may need. Once you have finished, estimate what you think each item will cost and go over your estimates with people who are knowledgeable in this area. Ask for clarification and constructive feedback. Also, comparison-shop so that you can get the most for your money. It's

also a good idea to estimate a little higher than what you actually need so that you will have enough money for your program. A rites of passage program can start at about $75,000 unless you are relying heavily on volunteers and donations.

Selling the Program to Your Organization

Depending on the culture of your organization and your relationship with your supervisor you will either; ask to meet with your supervisor to discuss your idea for an African-centered female rites of passage program then follow-up at a later date with a written proposal. Or, you will inform your supervisor that you've been conducting some research and based on your findings you believe that the organization will benefit from an African-centered female rites of passage program. Then tell him/her that you've drafted a program proposal and you would like him/her to review your proposal. If all goes well, the second step is to team up with your supervisor and discuss how you will sell the program idea upper to management in order to get organizational support. If your supervisor or upper management does not buy into the idea, ask for feedback, then adapt and modify your program and propose some variation of the program. If that does not work and your heart is set on offering this program, see if you can team up with a church or another group and offer the program independent of your organization.

Here are some tips for selling the program to key decision makers in your agency.

- Talk to key decision makers about how the program will benefit the overall organization.
- Talk to key decision makers about how it will increase the organization's ability to provide services to African-American clients in a culturally competent manner.
- Talk to key decision makers about how the program will compliment existing services.
- Talk to key decision makers about how the program can be used as a tool to obtain additional funding (including discretionary funds)
- Talk to key decision makers about how the program will provide the organization with the opportunity to be viewed as innovative and cutting-edge.

Recruiting Volunteers

A rites of passage program requires adequate adult support in order to be carried out effectively. One way to do this is to utilize volunteers to carry out specific functions. Volunteers should have clearly-defined roles, requirements and written job descriptions. Volunteers can be utilized to: provide one-on-one mentoring, collectively decide on the program content and format, recruit and select initiates, orientate other volunteers and parents, organize the initiation retreat and ceremony, lead other purpose-centered ceremonies, identify additional funding sources, fundraise or in any other capacity that enriches the overall rites program.

When identifying volunteers make sure that:

- They are interested in and able to work with African-American girls and young women in a culturally competent manner;
- They are mentally and emotionally stable;
- They are at least twenty-five years of age especially if your program services young women up to the age of twenty-one.
- They are able to make a long-term commitment (nine months to a year unless you are offering a condensed version of the program);
- They are motivated for service;
- They have a clear understanding or at least a healthy appreciation of African centered values, practices and principles;
- They are ready, willing and able to mentally and emotionally invest in the life of an African-American girl or young woman;
- They are dedicated to promoting sisterhood.

When selling the program to volunteers focus on benefits not features. Some of the benefits for volunteers are the program will allow them to: create positive change in the lives of African-American girls and young women, contribute to the community, form a sisterhood with other volunteers, learn traditional African-centered principles and practices, explore new career options, increase their personal and professional network and build an extended family.

You should provide potential volunteers with information on rites of passage programs and African-centered principles and traditional practices, as some will not be familiar with these concepts. At your general interest meeting you should provide potential volunteers with literature on the rites of passage process as well as suggested reading and resource lists. If you can get a copy of a video of a rites crossover ceremony, you may want to show it to potential volunteers so that they can get a clearer picture of the rites of passage process.

Getting Parents On Board

Parents are an integral part of the rites of passage program. Their support and participation makes their daughter's experience more meaningful. Parents can add to the success of your program in a variety of ways such as: chaperoning a field trip, helping with fundraising events, providing insight into their daughter's strengths and challenges, and designing outfits for the crossover ceremony. They can also encourage their daughters to follow through with your program requirements. Parents should not play a staff role in the program, because this may impede on their daughter's willingness to open up.

Mothers will often have a desire for their own rites of passage program. If possible, provide a mini rites of passage program for mothers in the context of a one or two-day workshop. Your activities and ceremonies should focus on the mothers' needs and challenges as they relate to supporting their daughters in the rites of passage process.

Here are some tips for selling the program to parents.

- Talk to parents about how the program will help their daughters to develop essential life skills.
- Talk to parents about how the program will help to improve relationships between daughters and their parents.
- Talk to parents about how the program will help their daughters to use their free time more wisely and how it will enable them to set personal, educational and career goals.
- Talk to parents about how the program will help their daughters to develop values that are often missing among today's youth.
- Talk to parents about how the program will help their daughters learn more about their cultural heritage.
- Alleviate any fears or concerns that parents may have about the program.
- Use parents of previous rites programs to talk about the benefits of the rites of passage program, even if they did not participate in your rites program.

Recruiting Initiates and Getting Their Buy-in

Most teenage girls and young women are not familiar with the structured rites of passage process. The whole idea may seem strange to them. This makes your task more difficult. Why? Because you will need to sell the program to potential initiates before they actually participate in it. One way to do this is through the development of an appealing recruitment message; one that is both motivational and catchy. Remember – what motivates adults may not motivate teenage girls, so you need to think out of the box and familiarize yourself with youth culture. Before you draft your motivational recruitment message, you need to know:

- What would motivate African-American females in your target age group to participate in your rites of passage program?
- Where can your target population be found?
- What do you need to say in your recruitment message to peak their interest?

Once you have answered these questions, you are ready to compose your recruitment message. Your recruitment message should be in the form of a flyer and should be posted in places where your intended population is usually found.

A recruitment message for teenage girls should be short, attention-grabbing, catchy and motivational. It should sell the program's benefits, not features. It should speak to the population that you are trying to reach. And most of all, it should leave them wanting to know more about your program.

Take a few moments to compose a recruitment message inviting potential initiates to a first-time general, interest meeting.

_____
_____
_____
_____
_____
_____
_____
_____
_____
_____
_____
_____
_____
_____
_____
_____
_____
_____
_____
_____
_____
_____
_____

In order for potential initiates to learn about your rites of passage program you need to publicize it. Here are some potential sources for promotion.

1) High Schools
2) Colleges
3) Community Centers
4) Sports/Recreational programs
5) Tenant's associations
6) Churches or mosques
7) Community boards
8) Libraries
9) Student organizations
10) Basketball courts
11) African-American associations and organizations
12) Women's associations and organizations
13) Game rooms
14) Street fairs
15) Street jams
16) Cultural arts centers
17) Nail salons
18) Beauty salons
19) Student development center
20) High school/college newspaper

When potential initiates come to your first meeting, they may not be sure why they are there. Some of them may have been encouraged to attend by their parents. Others may be tagging along with a friend and may have no real interest in participating in the program. Then there will be some who are generally interested in finding out what your program has to offer. Think of your first meeting as a general interest meeting and a pre-group screening process. The meeting should take place in the late afternoon, early evening or on the weekend so that potential initiates can easily attend. A meal should be served. The atmosphere should be structured, yet warm and friendly.

Here are some suggestions for selling the rites of passage program to potential initiates who attend the general interest meeting.

- Use teenage girls and young women who have been part of a rites of passage program to talk to potential initiates.
- Show video clips of other African-centered rites of passage ceremonies and activities.
- Talk to potential initiates about the rites of passage program being a special program that will give them the opportunity to build friendships, explore their career options and talk about anything that is on their minds.

- Talk to potential initiates about the rites of passage program providing them with tools to become successful young women.
- Find out what kinds of programs and services that the girls would be interested in participating in. The most important thing is to get the girls talking.

Although rare, sometimes you may have more girls interested in your program than you can actually accommodate. This is why it is essential that you limit your recruitment by selecting one or two avenues to target. During the first meeting you will also need to conduct a pre-group interview so that you can select the most appropriate young women for your program.

It is recommended that you limit the group size to no more than fifteen initiates. This number is small enough to foster group cohesion, yet large enough for maximum interaction. It is also recommended that you divide the participants by age. For example, if you get thirty to forty girls interested in participating in your program. You can run two separate groups; one for the younger girls and one for the older. This guidebook is written for service provides who are working with girls and young women between the ages of twelve and eighteen. If you are working with a different age group, then you can tweak out the program until it meets your needs. If you are working with a broad age group, it's a good idea to offer separate activities, at least some of the time. Why? Because if they are at different stages of development, they will have different needs and issues.

6

Administering the Rites of Passage Program

This chapter focuses on the nuts and bolts of carrying out an African-centered rites of passage program. By this point in the guidebook you have already completed most of the groundwork, so now you are prepared to administer and implement the program. The recommendations offered in this guidebook are based on a twelve-month program: Two months designated for planning and preparation and ten months for actual service delivery.

Generally, a rites of passage program runs between nine and twelve months and culminates with a crossover ceremony in which friends, family and other key adults in the community affirm the initiates new status and formally welcomes them into the community. In the African-centered female rites of passage program it is important that the women leading the program are of African heritage. Also, they should be familiar with African-centered principles, practices and values. This does not mean that women from other ethnic groups cannot participate. It means that if they do, they need to understand that they will be learning about and utilizing African-centered principles, practices and values.

Program Components

There are nine major components that make up the structured, African-centered rites of passage program. This section outlines each component and gives a brief description on how to implement it. Based on your organization's needs and resources you may wish to add additional components to your program or you may choose to do away with some of the components featured in this section.

Peer Group Rap Sessions

Once a week the initiates come together and participate in educational classes that focus on topics that impact their lives. Each session is about ninety minutes in length and should be co-facilitated by qualified adults. The goal of these sessions is to provide a non-judgmental and supportive environment where initiates can come together to develop and enhance life skills, explore issues that impact their lives, learn about their culture and take positive charge of their lives. A rap session curriculum is provided for you in the next chapter.

Independent Study

It is important that initiates learn about traditional African-centered practices as well as contributions that African-Americans made to this country. One way that they can learn this is through independent study. The more they know about who they are and where they come from, the less likely they are to buy into the negative messages and images aimed at them. I recommend that you assign two independent study assignments throughout the program year. Independent study can take place in the form of: an oral presentation, the reciting of a poem that reflects serious study of an African-American historical figure, or initiates can create a special project that focuses on a contribution that an African-American person made to our society.

Book club or Storytelling

You can decide to build in a book club or a storytelling circle as part of your rites of passage program. The book club requires that participants and group leaders read one book each quarter, preferably by an African-American author. After each reading, there should be a discussion focusing on what each person got out of the book. It is recommended that the book club meeting take place over tea and croissants or a formal luncheon and that participants dress up for the book club meetings. This serves two objectives. First, it provides a forum where initiates can learn proper social etiquette skills. Second, it increases their ability to move comfortably in a variety of social settings.

If a book club is not feasible for your program, you can offer a storytelling circle instead. Storytelling was a way that African-Americans passed on historical information, family traditions, and values. African and African-American folk tales often provide lessons on living with integrity and they also provide a historical framework for understanding how people of African ancestry viewed moral dilemmas. It's not so important that all the facts of the story are accurate, what is most important is that there's a lesson to the story, somewhat like a parable. A good storytelling circle will enable initiates to share important family traditions and it provides a vehicle for them to understand the importance of doing what is right.

Community Service

Community service is a key element of the African-centered rites of passage program. Historically, African-Americans are a communal people and it is essential that this is stressed to the younger generation. The value of community is expressed in one way or another in all of the principles of Nguzo Saba, particularly in the principles of Umoja (unity) and Ujima (collective work and responsibility). The community service component requires initiates to make a commitment of at least two hours per month to some form of community service which can include: tutoring younger children, providing errands and companionship for the elderly or homebound, donating and, or distributing food to a homeless shelter, visiting the sick, facilitating a neighborhood clean-up or anti-violence project, or any other project that helps others and fosters a sense of community.

Field Trips

Field trips provide participants with opportunities to expand their horizons and learn about the world. If possible, schedule field trips every other month to places such as: historical Black colleges, museums, spiritual institutions in order to see how different people worship, special cultural events, Kwanzaa celebrations, African-American bookstores and various other places of interest that initiates ordinarily may not go to.

Journals

At the start of the program each participant should be provided with a journal and encouraged to write in it daily. She should start the journal writing process by writing down at least five things that she is grateful for, afterwards she can write about anything she wants such as: her feelings, fear, hopes, dreams, goals and anything else she chooses to write. Initiates should also be encouraged to bring their journals to the rap sessions and share some of their writings. Keep in mind that journals are very personal, so participants should never be pressured to share anything that makes them feel uncomfortable.

Treasure Album

A treasure album contains pictures, letters, poetry, keepsakes, mementos and anything else that tells the story of the initiate's life. A treasure album is a photo album that initiates transform into a memorable keepsake by decorating it and placing things in it that hold special meaning for them. It is a pictorial method of recording one's life. Each participant is required to create one and they are displayed on a decorative table at the crossover ceremony.

Initiation Retreat

The initiation retreat is representative of the traditional African initiation rites activities where boys and girls were separated from each other and taken out of the village for a designated period of time in order to demonstrate their newly acquired skills and information so that they could be initiated into young adulthood. The initiation retreat should be held at a location other than where the initiates normally meet such as a camp site, dude ranch, bed and breakfast, retreat center or if permissible in an elder's home provided that there is adequate space. During the initiation retreat, initiates participate in a variety of activities and rituals developed by the elders in your rites program that test, reinforce and reaffirm everything that the initiates have learned. It is recommended that the initiation retreat take place over the course of a weekend to allow ample time for rituals and activities.

Crossover Ceremony

This special day marks that initiates have crossed over into young womanhood. It is the culmination of the work of initiates, their families and volunteers. This day highlights the accomplishments that the initiates have made during the program year and it formally introduces them into the community as young women. The initiates and elders dress in African garments and the initiates perform a rites of passage dance preferably to traditional African music. In addition, initiates can perform a group performance or initiates can perform solo acts such as: singing a song or reciting a poem. Each initiate should briefly discuss the significance of the program. Parents are also invited to speak about the significance of the program. You will need to limit the amount of parents that speak in order to stay within the time constraints of your program. Immediately following the ceremony food is served. Music, dance, prayer and ritual are all part of the program. At the conclusion of the ceremony, each participant is presented with a plaque and a homemade gift.

Clarifying Roles and Expectations for Rites of Passage Leaders, Parents and Mentors

In order to carry out a successful program, you need to make sure that all of the elders who are involved in your program have clearly-defined roles and understand what is expected of them. Elders include staff, parents, volunteers and any other adults who are actively involved in the rites program

Setting up an executive planning committee is one of the most important steps in this process. The committee can assist you in drafting the written proposal. Or, if you have already written the program proposal, the planning committee can assist by reviewing the proposal, making necessary adaptations and collectively deciding on the program's content and format. They can recruit, select, and orientate initiates, parents, additional volunteers, mentors and other people who may be participating in your rites of passage program. Although committee members will have specified roles, you should let them know, that they are expected to work together as a team and as such should pitch in wherever they are needed.

Following are some suggested roles and expectations for the committee members.

Project Director
Depending on your financial resources, this will either be a paid or voluntary position. The project director is responsible for:
- Leading the planning and development of the program.
- Preparing the agenda for administrative and, or board meetings.
- Coordinating the planning and implementation of all activities.

- Leading in the development of the program proposal.
- Overseeing the planning of the initiation retreat and the crossover ceremony.
- Reserving meeting space and making sure that refreshments are available for all meetings.
- Securing funding for program supplies and materials.

Assistant Project Director

The assistant director is responsible for:
- Performing all the duties of the project director in her absence.
- Assisting in all areas of program administration.
- Assisting with membership and recruitment.

Membership Coordinator

This may either be a paid or voluntary position. The membership coordinator is responsible for:
- Coordinating the recruitment of initiates, mentors and additional volunteers.
- Coordinating parent involvement activities.
- Orientating initiates, parents and mentors.
- Developing the agenda for parent, initiate and mentor meetings.

Treasurer/Fundraising Coordinator

The treasurer/fundraising coordinator is responsible for:
- Maintaining a record of expenses.
- Directing all fundraising events.
- Obtaining requisition checks and distributing funds to the appropriate people.
- Writing letters to corporate sponsors for donations and, or funding.
- Developing a working budget for the rites program.

Rap Session Co-facilitators

These two positions may either be paid or voluntary, but they need to be carried out by qualified adults who have experience and training in facilitating adolescent groups. The rap session co-facilitators are responsible for:
- Developing the rap session curriculum.
- Leading the sessions.
- Maintaining session notes.
- Making appropriate referrals.
- Leading the book club/storytelling circles.
- Overseeing the development of the treasure albums.
- Brining in guest speakers to speak to the initiates during the rap session segment.

Secretary
The secretary is responsible for:
- Taking minutes at all meetings.
- Reminding initiates of meeting via telephone, mail or e-mail.
- Composing flyers, messages and announcements.

Activities Coordinator
The activities coordinator is responsible for:
- Maintaining a written and pictorial record of program activities.
- Chaperoning field trips.
- Coordinating community service activities.

The suggested roles and expectations are presented to assist you. But you do what you need to do to make your program work. Sometimes because of organizational constraints, one person may have to carry out more than one role. It is not recommended, but knowing the limited resources that many human service organizations have, this is something that you may have to consider in order to get you program off the ground.

In terms of organizing the initiation retreat and crossover ceremony, I suggest that you approach these tasks from a team perspective. Rather than assigning one person to plan both events, get input from initiates and parents and collectively organize and plan the initiation retreat and crossover ceremony. You will need one person to spearhead the process and coordinate everyone's efforts.

Additional Roles and Responsibilities

Parents
Parents, and or parent-figures are a key component of the program. They are expected to attend the orientation and parents meetings. They are expected to support initiates by offering encouragement and guidance. They are expected to support the program by making sure that their daughters follow through on all program requirements. And when appropriate, parents should be encouraged to chaperon filed trips. Parents can also assist with the preparation of the crossover ceremony, designing garments and preparing food. Do not underestimate the importance of parent involvement. Parents have skills and resources that can significantly add to the program.

Mentors
Mentoring is an important aspect of the rites of passage program. Mentors play several roles. They offer coaching, guidance, an empathic ear, friendship, wisdom and so much more. No matter how close a girl is with her mother, she will not tell her everything. A mentor should be able to fill in some of those gaps. There should be one mentor for every initiate so that one-to-one bonding can take place. It is strongly advised that mentors are at least seven years older

than their mentees, so that the relationship is one of elder to initiate rather than peer to peer. The role that a mentor plays in an initiate's life can range from getting together once a month to do special things together, to talking on the phone once a week about issues that are of importance to the initiate. You will need to determine how much of a time commitment that you would like mentors to make. Keep in mind that many of the mentors will have full-time jobs and families of their own, therefore their time is usually limited. It is a good idea to have a written role description and time commitment agreement so that mentors are clear about what you need from them. It is also recommended that you develop a mentor's application and have a screening process in place.

Utilizing A Time-line to Organize Tasks

I strongly encourage you to develop a projected time-line that outlines the tasks you need to accomplish from start to finish. The time line should include the work you need to do from the development phase of your rites program all the way to the crossover ceremony. A time-line is a useful tool, because it enables you to prioritize tasks and manage the flow of work. Following is a sample time-line. It reflects a twelve-month rites of passage program *(nine months of actual programming, three months of development)*. If you are offering a condensed version of the program, you can make the necessary adjustments in order to meet your program's needs.

1st Month
- Gather information about African-centered female rites of passage programs.
- Conduct a needs analysis and develop a written proposal or concept paper.
- Obtain organizational support.
- Identify executive committee members and meet with the committee.

2nd Month
- Develop program promotional materials.
- Identify and reach out to corporate sponsors.
- Develop a program curriculum or review the one that I have provided for you and make modifications to meet your program's needs.
- Recruit initiates, mentors and other volunteers.
- Hold committee meeting.

3rd Month
- Orientate initiates, mentors parents and all other key people.
- Match initiates with mentors.

- Begin peer group rap sessions.
- Set up initiate community service projects.
- Hold committee meeting.

4th Month

- Continue peer group rap sessions.
- Schedule a field trip.
- Assign initiates their first book and hold a book club meeting at the end of the month.
- Hold committee meeting.

5th Month

- Assign initiates their independent study assignments.
- Continue peer group rap sessions.
- Evaluate program progress (Formally or informally find out from initiates, their parents, staff and mentors what's working and what's not)
- Hold committee meeting.

6th Month

- Continue peer group rap sessions.
- Begin planning the initiation retreat and crossover ceremony.
- Schedule a field trip.
- Hold committee meeting.

7th Month

- Continue peer group rap sessions.
- Assign initiates their second book and hold a book club meeting at the end of the month.
- Hold committee meeting.

8th Month

- Continue peer group rap sessions.
- Look for a retreat site.
- Schedule a field trip.
- Evaluate program progress.
- Decide on theme, color schemes and outfits to be worn for the crossover ceremony.
- Talk to initiates about creating a dance for the crossover ceremony.
- Hold committee meeting.

9th Month

- Continue peer group rap sessions.
- Secure retreat site and space for the crossover ceremony, unless the crossover ceremony will be held at your organization.
- Write to organizations and request donations for the initiation retreat such as: journals, ceremonial tools, self-care products, magazines, CD's and any other items that would enhance this special event.
- Develop activities for the initiation retreat.
- Hold committee meeting.

10th Month

- Continue peer group rap sessions.
- Assign initiates their third book and hold a book club meeting at the end of the month.
- Schedule a field trip.
- Plan the agenda for the initiation retreat and crossover ceremony. This should include entertainment, guest speakers and the overall agenda.
- Initiates should check in to make sure that they are up to date on all of your graduation requirements.
- Initiates who have not met your graduation requirements are given an opportunity to do supplementary work.
- Send out invitations for the crossover ceremony.
- Secure transportation for the retreat.
- Hold committee meeting.

11th Month

- Continue peer group rap sessions.
- Follow-up on invitations that were sent out last month.
- Secure supplies and final details for the initiation retreat and crossover ceremony.
- Hold initiation retreat.
- Hold committee meetings (by the 11th month the committee will probably need to meet bi-weekly to secure all of the details for the retreat and crossover ceremony).

12th Month

- Continue peer group rap sessions.
- Evaluate program.
- Prepare menu for the crossover ceremony.
- Confirm everyone's attendance.
- Hold crossover ceremony.

Program Requirements

It is important that you set clear expectations for the initiates right from the start. They need to know what is expected of them and what they are supposed to do in order to participate in your rites program and crossover. When you hold your first committee meeting, it is a good idea to collectively establish what the program requirements will be and put them in writing. During the orientation go over the requirements with initiates and answer all questions that arise. You should also provide parents with a letter outlining the graduation requirements.

Guiding Principles and Codes

Since the rites of passage program outlined in this book is geared for African-American girls and young women, the guiding principles and codes are African-centered. This enables, initiates, mentors, staff, parents and all other involved parties to learn about and practice traditional African-centered values, principles and customs. In many structured African-centered rites of passage programs the seven principles of Nguzo Saba, *(principles that are commonly associated with Kwanzaa)* or the code of MAAT *(seven virtues rooted in Egyptology)* serve as the foundation for the program. Presented here are the principles of Nguzo Saba and the code of MAAT.

The Seven Principles of Nguzo Saba

Founded by Dr. Maulana Karenga in 1966, these principles have been practiced throughout the African Diaspora to connect and empower people of African ancestry. The principles of Nugzo Saba are meant to guide, empower and connect people of African ancestry individually and collectively. The key to helping initiates understand these principles and apply them is to show them how they can and are at work in their daily lives. Following are the seven principles of Nguzo Saba:

1) Umoja (Unity)
To strive for and maintain unity in the family, community nation and race living together in peace and harmony. One way to help parents and initiates understand how unity can work in their daily lives is to encourage them to have meals together and to make meal time family discussion time. Another way to help initiates practice the principle of unity is by designing activities that encourage relationship building.

2) Kujichagulia (Self-determination)

To create opportunities to name ourselves, define ourselves create for ourselves, speak for ourselves and make our own decisions instead of being defined, named, created for and spoken for by others. One way to help initiates understand and practice self-determination is by allowing them to name their group. Another way is to get their input and incorporate it into the rites program.

3) Ujima (Collective Work and Responsibility)

To build and maintain our community, with everyone working together and make our sister's and brother's problems our problems and work to solve them together. The community service component will enable initiates to understand and practice collective work and responsibility. By contributing to the community, initiates learn the value of giving back and helping others in need.

4) Ujamaa (Cooperative Economics)

To build and maintain our own stores, shops and other businesses and to profit from them together. An effective way to teach initiates about cooperative economics is to schedule guided field trips to Black owned businesses and historically Black colleges. This way they learn to see entrepreneurship as a career option and they learn the importance of investing in their communities.

5) Nia (Purpose)

To make our collective vocation the building and developing of our communities in order to restore our people to their traditional greatness. Workshops around goal setting are an effective way to help initiates develop a sense of purpose. Before they can assist in the building and developing of their communities, they must build and develop themselves. Another way to help initiates discover their purpose is by having them write out a purpose statement.

6) Kuumba (Creativity)

To do as much as we can, in the way that we can to leave our communities more beautiful and beneficial than we inherited them. Creativity is always at work among adolescents. Through the cultural arts, creative expression, volunteerism and any other vehicle of positive self-expression, initiates should be encourage to be creative. Find out what special talent each initiate has and encourage the development of that talent.

7) Imani (Faith)

To believe with all our heart in our people, our parents, our teachers, our leaders and the righteousness and victory of our struggle. One way to encourage initiates to build their faith is through a testimonial circle. A testimonial circle is a group of people gathered in a circle who each give a testimony of how they've overcome what seemed impossible, faced a difficult challenge, came through a difficult situation, showed courage during a crisis, or had a prayer answered. By hearing other people's stories of triumph and success initiates are able to build their faith.

The Code of MAAT

MAAT is based on Egyptology. According to the ancient Egyptians MAAT is the intuitive sense of order that comes from within. It is believed by the ancients that when we pass from physical life to everlasting spiritual life MAAT is the code upon which our lives will be measured. It is believed that if one practices the code of MAAT in their daily interactions with others, then he or she will reap the benefits of a more balanced, harmonious and prosperous life. No matter what spiritual path one takes, the code of MAAT is a governing force.

1) Truth
To seek truth, speak truth, teach truth and accept truth lovingly and consistently.

2) Righteousness
To do what is right in order to create balance and harmony for all. To exemplify integrity.

3) Justice
To treat yourself and others equitably. To treat others as you would have them treat you.

4) Harmony
To think and act in ways that manifest peace, cooperation and accord.

5) Balance
To strive for stability and a state of equilibrium.

6) Propriety
To be humble and speak with a conscious tongue. To display an attitude of gratitude

7) Order
To be organized and clear. To be consciously aware that there is a divine system that governs the universe and everything that exists within it.

7

Facilitating the Rap
Session Curriculum

The rap session curriculum outlined in this book offers forty-two sessions in all. There are thirty, 90-minute structured sessions and twelve open sessions *(sessions that you will develop yourself)*. Feel free to modify the curriculum as you see fit. School vacations and holidays were taken into consideration in the design of this curriculum.

There are seven session areas presented in this curriculum. The session areas are consistent with the seven principles of Nguzo Saba. Depending on the nature and demographics of your program, you may want to add additional session areas. This is perfectly fine. Following are the seven session areas presented in this curriculum.

1. Unity (umoja)

2. Self-determination (Kujichagulia)

3. Collective Work and Responsibility (Ujima)

4. Cooperative Economics (Ujamaa)

5. Purpose (Nia)

6. Creativity (Kuumba)

7. Faith (Imani)

Essentials for Group Success

A team of two skilled and experienced facilitators is preferable, because this allows for mutual support, continuity, balance, different leadership styles and it models the skill of teamwork. As mentioned earlier, the group size should be limited to fifteen initiates. Also, it is recommended that you hold the group rap sessions on a weekly basis. If weekly sessions are not feasible for your group, you can meet bi-weekly.

- **Group Setting**
  The group should be held in a private room where other people will not be able to overhear what is being discussed in the group. It is best to hold the rap sessions in a room with a door that can be closed and you should post a *"group in session, do not disturb"* sign on the door. The group should sit in a circle, since a circle is symbolic of all parts being equal. Chairs should be arranged in a circle before the initiates enter the room. You should also provide refreshments. I believe that refreshments are an important element in the African-centered rites of passage program, because food is an integral part of African and African-American culture.

- **Establish Clear Expectations**
  It is essential that the group facilitators establish a set of ground rules for the group from the very first meeting. Ground rules can be developed by the entire group; with the understanding that facilitators will make the final decision. It is a good idea to set ground rules for: conduct within the sessions, confidentiality, time and attendance. Facilitators should make sure that they model the kind of behavior that they expect from initiates.

- **Creating A Safe Environment**
  In all group settings, safety is an essential ingredient for successful group work. Because initiates come from different walks of life, they may not automatically trust the group leaders or each other. The trust level needs to be nurtured and encouraged. Safety can be established through confidentiality, consistency, open communication and clear expectations.

- **Group Cohesion**
  Another important aspect of successful group work is fostering a sense of group cohesion. Members need to feel like they are working together towards a common purpose. Group cohesion is what unites group members and fosters a sense of teamwork. As a result of doing activities together and sharing feelings and ideas, a sense of cohesion will begin to develop.

Session Area 1.

Unity

The Nguzo Saba defines unity as: striving for and maintaining unity within members of a family, community, nation and race living together in peace and harmony.

The sessions in this area are designed to instill the principle of unity in initiates through relationship building skills and community building activities.

Building A Village

Objectives

To help initiates get to know each other and gain comfort in the group setting. To establish ground rules for the group. To identify why initiates want to be part of the rites program, what they hope to contribute and what they would like to get out of the program.

Materials

Flipchart, construction paper, markers and scissors

Process

1. Welcome initiates and go over the objectives of the overall program and this particular session.
2. Distribute construction paper, markers and scissors. Ask each initiate to outline her hand on a piece of paper. Next, ask initiates to write their names in the palm of their paper hands and on each finger write: something that they like about themselves, something they want to share with the group, something they hope to get out of the group, what they like to do in their spare time, and their favorite movie or book. When they are finished, have everyone place their paper hands in a box or bag. Shake it well then ask everyone to pick a hand. If an initiate gets her own paper hand, have her pick again.
3. Next, ask everyone to pair up with the person whose hand they picked and get acquainted (about 10 minutes). When everyone is finished, have each pair introduce her partner to the group and share what she learned about her.
4. Model this activity by introducing your partner first.
5. Talk to the group about the importance of ground rules for the success of a village. Point out that ground rules help all members to be valued, respected and heard. Suggest a few basic ground rules then ask members to brainstorm and come up with ground rules for the village (rap session group). Write their responses on the flipchart.
6. Ask initiates to pair up with their partners again and respond to the following questions:
   - What does sisterhood mean to you?
   - What are some ways that girls and young women can show each other that they are sisters?
7. Ask initiates to share their responses with the entire group. Give appropriate feedback and say something positive about each girl.
8. Ask initiates if there is anything that they would like to share before the session ends and remind them of the next session.

What Is A Family?

Objectives
To help initiates explore what family means to them. To help initiates become comfortable sharing personal information with the group. To help initiates recognize that they are not alone in dealing with difficult family issues.

Materials
Flipchart, pens, paper and journals.

Process
1. Briefly go over the objectives for this session.
2. Ask group members to respond to the following sentence stems on a sheet of paper.
   - Family to me means ....
   - The role of the mother in a family is ....
   - The role of the father in a family is.........
   - The role of the daughter in a family is ......
   - My family provides me with ....
   - I provide my family with........
   - The other people who I consider my family are.......
3. Have initiates discuss their responses with the group, record them on the flipchart and provide appropriate feedback.
4. Explain that the word "family" means different things to different people and explain that one way to define family is two or more people who have an ongoing relationship and strive to nurture each other and meet one another's needs. Ask them to think about people in their lives who fit this definition and have them write their names in the journals that you have provided for them.
5. Invite initiates to raise questions or share reactions to what you have discussed thus far. Provide appropriate feedback.
6. Tell the group that everyone will now have the opportunity to create small families within the group. Pair initiates up into groups of three to five people, and find an area in the room where they can sit in a private circle. Tell them to take 5 minutes to decide what kind of family they want to be and give everyone a name, a role and an age.
7. Tell them to pretend that they've just received a letter from a long, lost relative who is coming to visit the family tomorrow. This long, lost relative used to be sad because he/she thought that he/she didn't have any family and now he/she has found all of you.
8. Ask them to role play in their groups for about 10 minutes on what they will say and do as a family to let this relative know that he/she is not alone.

9. After 10 minutes stop the role play and ask each group to share how their family plans to let the relative know that he/she is not alone.

10. Discuss the following questions.
   - What did you learn about how family members make decisions when they come together?
   - Was it difficult or easy for your family to work together in order to come to a decision? Why or why not?
   - How do you think the information you learned today could help you in understanding and dealing with your own family?

11. Ask initiates if there is anything they would like to share before the session ends and remind them of the next session.

My Family Road Map

Objectives

To help initiates create a visual representation of their family and explore their family relationships. To help initiates begin to collect important data about their families so they will have a clearer picture of where they come from.

Materials

Newsprint, markers, a diagram of your state's road signs or a copy of the driver's manual, and genealogy handouts.

Process

1. Briefly go over the objectives for this session
2. Explain that part of the session will take place today, the other part will be an independent study project that they will be required to hand in at a later date.
3. Introduce the concept of a family map by explaining that a family map is a visual way to get important information about one's family.
4. Lead initiates in a short visualization to help them focus on their relationships with their family. They should include their biological families as will as their chosen ones. Tell them to think about the kinds of relationships they have with each family member. Are they close? Distant? Strained? Broken?
5. Distribute newsprint and markers. Then provide instructions for drawing a family map, using yourself as an example by creating your family map for all the initiates to see.
6. Ask initiates to draw their family maps, writing their name in the middle of the paper and drawing a circle around it. Then instruct them to draw a circle representing each person in their family with one adjective that describes that person's role in the family and one adjective to describe their relationship with that person. Next, instruct initiates to draw signpost to symbolize the type of relationship that they have with each family member. For example, they can draw a merging traffic sign to symbolize close, positive bonds. They can draw a two-way traffic sign to indicate healthy, but less intimate connections. They can draw a yield sign to symbolize strained relationships. They can draw a dead end or a stop sign to symbolize disconnected relationships. They can use any signpost that they choose as long as they can clearly express how it symbolizes their family relationships. You will need to have pictures of road signs displayed for all to see.
7. After they have finished, ask initiates to share their family road maps with the group. Give appropriate feedback. Note - this activity may bring up strong feelings. Allow time to deal with issues as they arise.

7.   After they have finished, ask initiates to share their family road maps with the group. Give appropriate feedback. Note - this activity may bring up strong feelings. Allow time to deal with issues as they arise.

8.   End the session with a discussion of how initiates can use their family road maps as a visual way for understanding themselves in relation to their families and as a tool for building healthier family relationships.

9.   Ask initiates if there is anything they would like to share before the session ends.

10.   Go over the genealogy handout on the following page, distribute it and explain to initiates that they will be working on the genealogy handout independently. Set a due date for it to be completed and have them place it in their treasure albums. Point out to initiates that they may not be able to get all of the information requested in the genealogy handout, but to complete as much as they can.

Genealogy Handout

Mother's Genealogy

Initiate's Name _____
Date of Birth _____ Place of Birth_____

Parents

Mother _____   Father_____
Date and Place of Birth_____   Date and Place of Birth_____

Grandparents

Maternal   Paternal

Grandmother _____   Grandmother_____
Date and Place of Birth_____   Date and Place of Birth_____
Grandmother_____   Grandfather_____
Date and Place of Birth _____   Date & Place of Birth_____

Great Grandparents

Maternal   Paternal

Great Grandmother_____   Great Grandmother_____
Date and Place of Birth_____   Date and Place of Birth_____
Great Grandmother_____   Great Grandmother_____
Date and Place of Birth_____   Date and Place of Birth_____

Genealogy Handout

Father's Genealogy

Initiate's Name _____
Date of Birth _____ Place of Birth_____

Parents

Mother _____   Father_____
Date and Place of Birth _____   Date and Place of Birth_____

Grandparents

Maternal   Paternal

Grandmother_____   Grandmother_____
Date and Place of Birth_____   Date and Place of Birth_____
Grandmother_____   Grandfather_____
Date and Place of Birth_____   Date and Place of Birth_____

Great Grandparents

Maternal   Paternal

Great Grandmother_____   Great Grandmother_____
Date and Place of Birth_____   Date and Place of Birth_____
Great Grandfather_____   Great Grandfather_____
Date and Place of Birth_____   Date and Place of Birth_____

Building A Sister Circle

Objectives
To help initiates build healthy female friendships. To help initiates identify negative friendship behaviors and replace them with more positive ones. To encourage initiates to make new friends and develop stronger bonds with the ones they have.

Materials
Roll of paper and markers

Process
1. Briefly go over the objectives for this session.
2. Ask for four volunteers from the group. Instruct two of the volunteers to lie down on the paper while the other two draw outlines of their bodies. Have two more volunteers tape the body outlines on the wall and write the words "positive friendship behaviors" on one and "negative friendship behaviors" on the other.
3. Have initiates brainstorm for each list and ask two different volunteers to write their responses on the body outlines.
4. Facilitate a discussion around negative and positive friendship behaviors and ask initiates to identify some things that females can do to build healthier relationships with one another.
5. Ask initiates to pretend that they are placing an ad for a good friend in their favorite magazine. Instruct them to write a few sentences describing what they have to offer a good friend and a few sentences describing what they are looking for in a good friend. When they are finished, have them place their ads in a box or bag and ask each initiate to pick an ad. If an initiate picks her own ad have her put it back and select again. Ask each initiate to read the ad that she selected and discuss why she would make a good friend for the person who wrote the ad.
6. Give appropriate feedback and encourage initiates to get to know one of the other initiates more deeply before the next session by talking on the phone or doing something special together.
7. Ask members if there is anything they would like to share before the session ends. Remind them of the next session.

Developing Healthy Relationships With Males

Objectives
To help initiates develop healthier relationship with males. To help initiates recognize the difference between a healthy, nurturing relationship and an unhealthy, addictive one. To help initiates set appropriate boundaries with their male peers

Materials
Flipchart, index cards, pens, articles from an advice column that deal with relationship issues.

Process
1. Briefly go over the objectives for this session
2. Ask members to think of a popular song in which the theme is "love or relationships." Ask them in what ways does the song that they selected reflect the current state of relationships between young males and females. Write their responses on the flipchart. Give appropriate feedback.
3. Ask members to brainstorm and create two lists, one that describes the characteristics of a healthy relationship and one that describes the characteristics of an unhealthy one. Give appropriate feedback.
4. Divide members into three groups and give each group a relationship advice article with the expert's advice taken out. Have each group respond to their article and ask them to write their advice on the index card.
5. When members are finished, have them read their article aloud and share their advice with the entire group. Ask group members to give feedback.
6. Conclude by reiterating the characteristics of a healthy relationship and pointing out the importance of setting boundaries. Ask members if there is anything they would like to share before the session ends.

Session 6.

Suggested Topics

Following are suggested topics for continued work in the area of unity.
Mother and Daughter Relationships, Father and Daughter Relationships,
Dating Violence, Love and Intimacy and Assessing Your Relationship Readiness

Topic_____

Objectives

_____
_____
_____
_____

Materials

_____
_____

Process

_____
_____
_____
_____
_____
_____
_____
_____
_____
_____
_____
_____
_____
_____
_____
_____
_____
_____
_____
_____
_____

The Nguzo Saba defines self-determination as: to create opportunities to define ourselves, name ourselves, create for ourselves and speak for ourselves instead of being defined, named, created for and spoken for by others.

The sessions in this area are designed to instill the principle of self-determination in initiates through the promotion of self-awareness, self-respect and self-responsibility.

The Me I See

Objectives

To help initiates develop a more positive view of themselves. To help initiates identify their positive qualities and traits. To help initiates identify areas in their lives that they need to work on.

Materials

Index cards, paper and pens.

Process

1. Briefly go over the objectives for this session.

2. Ask initiates to divide a sheet of paper in half and create one column that states "what I love about myself," and one column that states "what I need to work on."

3. Have them pair up and share their lists. Ask them to offer their partner some positive actions steps for at least two items in the category entitled, "what I need to work on." Have each pair share their list with the entire group. Ask the rest of the group to write down two positive things about each person on the index cards and hand it to them when they are finished reporting out.

4. During the session, encourage members to counteract negative statements that initiates make about themselves.

5. Conclude the session by pointing out that when people feel bad about themselves they often behave in counterproductive ways and that the only way to stop feeling bad about yourself is to love, value and accept who you are.

6. Ask members if there is anything they would like to share before the session ends.

The Many Faces of Me

Objectives
To help initiates develop a clearer sense of identity. To teach initiates the skills of self-reflection and personal inventory.

Materials
Paper and pens

Process
1. Briefly go over the objectives for this session.
2. Give initiates a sheet of paper and ask them to divide it into five categories: physical, intellectual, spiritual, emotional and social. Ask them to describe themselves by writing three words that identify who they are in each category. Once members are finished, ask them to pair up with someone in the group, share one word from each category and explain why that word describes who they are.
3. Reassemble the larger group and ask.
   - What category was most difficult for you to write and talk about? Why?
   - What category do you feel most confident about and why?
   - How are the different categories connected?
   - What did you learn about yourself that you didn't realize before?
   - What category do you want to grow stronger in and what is one step that you can take to strengthen it?
4. Provide appropriate feedback sharing positive observations about each member.
5. Ask members if there is anything they would like to share before the session ends.

Accepting Responsibility

Objectives

To help initiates hold themselves accountable for the choices that they make. To help initiates realize that while they cannot control everything that happens to them, they have the power to control how they respond.

Materials

Paper and pens

Process

1. Briefly go over the objectives for this session.
2. Discuss what it means to be responsible and ask members to write about a time they behaved responsibly and a time they did not behave responsibly when they should have. Ask them to share their responses with the group.
3. Give positive feedback for the time they accepted responsibility and ask the other group members to offer suggestions for ways the individual could have been more responsible, during the time when they did not accept appropriate responsibility.
4. Present the idea that we have a choice about how happy and successful we can be, by accepting responsibility for our thoughts and actions. Even if we come from a painful past, we do not have to allow what happened to us to determine where we end up in life.
5. Invite initiates to identify one way that they can exercise their personal power and become more responsible.
6. Ask initiates if there is anything they would like to share before the session ends.

Respecting Yourself and Others

Objectives
To help initiates learn how to behave more respectfully towards themselves and others. To help initiates understand the difference between appropriate and inappropriate behavior.

Materials
Flipchart, paper and pens, pre-recorded videotape of popular musical videos.

Process
1. Briefly go over the objectives for this session.
2. Ask initiates to define the word respect. Record their responses on the flipchart and give appropriate feedback on a sheet of paper.
3. Ask initiates to respond to the following sentence stems.
   - I show myself that I respect myself by ....
   - I show others that I respect myself by ....
   - I show others that I respect them by ....
   - When I feel disrespected I usually...........
   - If I disrespect someone else I feel...........
   - I take responsibility for my behavior by ....
   - I let others know what my boundaries are by.......
4. Have initiates discuss their responses with the group, record them on the flipchart and provide appropriate feedback.
5. Show the group about ten minutes of your video tape featuring popular music videos and ask them the following questions.
   - What messages do you get about people respecting each other?
   - Do you think people respect each other as much as they did during your parents' generation? Why or why not?
   - Do you believe that females are disrespected in popular music videos? Why or why not?
   - What kind of messages do videos give about African American young women respecting themselves and each other?
6. Give appropriate feedback and point out that respect is essential in building healthy families, relationships with peers, relationships with people at work and strong communities.
7. Ask initiates if there is anything they would like to share before the session ends. Ask initiates to bring their journals for the next session.

Living With Integrity

Objectives
To help initiates develop an internal moral code of conduct to guide their daily decisions. To help initiates use positive affirmations to create their desired mental state.

Materials
Flipchart, journals, pens, self-addressed stamped post cards

Process
1. Briefly go over the objectives for this session.
2. Define the word integrity, then ask the group to write down three women who they know personally or through the media who they believe are living a life to integrity. These are women who stand up for what they believe is right and are examples of people who are honest, ethical and understanding. Point out that while no one is perfect, there are people who try to do the right thing despite what other people think. When they are finished, have them share their responses and give appropriate feedback.
3. Ask each initiate to write down three integrity rules that she tries to live by and describe why these rules are important to her.
4. Ask each initiate to share one of her integrity rules with the group and discuss how this rule guides her daily decisions.
5. Ask initiates to brainstorm and come up with additional integrity rules that would be helpful for the entire group.
6. Discuss the concept of affirmations *(positive things that you say to yourself to build your self-worth and create your desired mental state)*
7. Ask each initiate to say a positive affirmation about herself and write it on her post card.
8. Collect the post cards and inform initiates that you will mail the post cards on your way home so that they will receive them before the next session.
9. Tell initiates to look out for their post card and when it arrives tape it on the mirror and recite it everyday.
10. Inform initiates that this exercise may seem strange at first, but the more they affirm themselves, the better they will feel about themselves. Additionally, the more they affirm who they are, the more they will be able to live by their integrity rules. Ask initiates if there is anything they would like to share before the session ends.

Suggested Topics

Following are suggested topics for continued work in the area of self-determination.
Handling Put Downs and Criticism, Choices and Consequences, Dealing With Feelings and My Rights as a Person

Topic_____

Objectives

_____
_____
_____
_____

Materials

_____
_____
_____

Process

_____
_____
_____
_____
_____
_____
_____
_____
_____
_____
_____
_____
_____
_____
_____
_____
_____
_____
_____
_____

Session Area 3.

Collective Work and Responsibility

The Nguzo Saba defines collective work and responsibility as: to build and maintain our community together and make our sister's and brother's problems our problems and to solve them together.

The sessions in this area are designed to instill the principle of collective work and responsibility in initiates through teamwork, effective communication and community service.

Being A Team Player

Objectives
To help initiates learn the benefits of teamwork. To help initiates learn that teamwork is a necessary tool for building successful relationships and communities. To help initiates identify personal barriers to successful team work.

Materials
Flipchart, ten newspapers, four rolls of masking tape, paper and pens.

Process
1. Briefly go over the objectives for this session.
2. Ask group to identify the characteristics of a successful team and record their responses on the flipchart
3. Instruct the group that they are going to build a tower. Divide initiates into three groups. One group will construct the tower in silence, the second group will provide directions for the builders, the third group will silently observe the dynamics that occur between the other two groups and write their observations on paper.
4. Provide the builders with a pile of newspapers and four rolls of masking tape and instruct them to build a tower out of the newspaper and tape that is six feet high, freestanding with three points touching the floor. Instruct the second group to come up with a strategy to help the builders construct the tower. Once they have devised their strategy, they can direct the builders in constructing the tower. The builders cannot speak to the directors or each other. They may only listen for cues and instructions. Give the groups 30 minutes to complete the task.
5. Instruct the observers to look for the following: roles that emerge within the groups, style of interaction, personal and social barriers to successful teamwork and the group's strengths as a whole.
6. After 30 minutes instruct observers to give their feedback. Then have the other groups give a self-assessment.
7. Ask the entire group the following questions.
   - In what way was this exercise similar to real life experiences that people have when they work together in a group?
   - What was the most challenging aspect of this exercise?
   - What did you learn about yourself?
   - What did you learn about the other young ladies?
   - Do you feel like you were successful?
   - What could have been done differently in order for you to have a more successful team experience?

8. Provide appropriate feedback and instruct participants to try again, this time with everyone working together as a team.

9. Reiterate the characteristics of a successful team that you recorded on the flipchart and discuss the importance of teamwork in building successful relationships and communities.

10. Ask initiates if there is anything they would like to share before the session ends.

Assertive Communication

Objectives
To help initiates develop effective communication skills. To help initiates recognize how they communicate with others.

Materials
Paper and pens

Process
1. Briefly go over the objectives for this session.
2. Define the words: assertive, aggressive, and passive-aggressive. Point out that these are the three ways the people interact and communicate with one another.
3. Divide initiates into three groups and have them write down one example of each communication style. Have each group share their examples and provide appropriate feedback.
4. Assign each group a style of communication and have them come up with a role play that depicts the assigned style of communication. Give appropriate feedback. Discuss which responses were most effective and why.
5. Then ask the entire group the following questions.
   - Which style of communication do you tend to use most often?
   - Which response do you believe is most effective and why?
   - How can you learn to be more assertive?
6. Conclude by discussing the benefits of assertive communication.
7. Ask initiates if there is anything they would like to share before the session ends.

Making Smart Decisions

Objectives

To help initiates develop effective decision making skills. To help initiates learn how to implement the five-step decision making strategy when faced with difficult decisions. To help initiates better understand how one's values and self-esteem impact on their decisions.

Materials

Pens and Paper

Process

1. Briefly go over the objectives for this session.
2. Introduce the activity by asking initiates to think about a time when they had to make a difficult decision. Ask them to write down what the dilemma was and what was the outcome. Have them share their response with the group. Provide appropriate feedback.
3. Focus on a recent media issue where a public figure had to make a difficult decision. Ask members to share their feelings regarding the incident and what steps do they think were involved in the public figure making his/her decision.
4. Explain that there is a five-step strategy that will enable them to make better decisions. This strategy consists of: examining the choices, gathering all of the details, weighing the pros and cons, examining the final consequences and making the decision. Ask the group to refer back to their difficult decision and share what steps they used in determining a final decision.
5. Ask the group the following questions.
   - What affects a person's ability to make smart decisions?
   - How does one's values affect their decisions?
   - How does one's self-esteem level affect their decisions?
   - Have you ever made a decision just to fit in with the crowd or please someone else?
   - How can people learn from bad decisions?
6. Conclude the session by reiterating the importance of thinking a situation through before making a hasty decision.
7. Ask initiates if there is anything they would like to share before the session ends.

The Making of A Leader

Objectives

To help initiates develop leadership skills. To help initiates identify ways that they can display leadership in their families, with peers and in their communities.

Materials

Flipchart, a bowling ball, pre-selected 20 minute scene of the movie "Soul Food"

Process

1. Briefly go over the objectives for this session.
2. Ask initiates to brainstorm on the qualities of an effective leader. Record their responses on the flipchart.
3. Instruct initiates to sit in a circle on the floor. Explain that you will be using the bowling ball to illustrate the heavy responsibility of being a leader. Roll the ball to one initiate, then let initiates roll it among themselves for a while.
4. Ask the group the following questions.
   - How is the weight of the ball similar to the weight of being a leader?
   - What could happen if you felt so weighed down that you dropped the ball?
   - What could be done to make sure that the ball isn't dropped?
5. Show 20 minutes of the movie, "Soul Food" and ask participants to give examples of how leadership skills were displayed throughout the family.
6. Ask initiates to provide examples of how they display leadership in their families, with peers and in their communities.
7. Ask initiates if there is anything that they would like to share before the session ends. Ask them to bring their journals for the next session.

The Cycle of Reciprocity

Objectives

To help initiates learn about the importance of community service. To help initiates understand the importance of performing random acts of kindness without expecting anything in return.

Materials

Flipchart, journals, assorted construction paper, glitter, gift boxes, glue, ribbon

Process

1. Briefly go over the objectives for this session.

2. Introduce the activity by asking initiates to brainstorm on the benefits of giving back to the community. Some of their responses may be: gain satisfaction from helping others, learn new skills, meet new people, create positive change, etc. Record their responses on a flipchart. Give appropriate feedback.

3. Ask initiates to recall a time they did something nice for someone without expecting anything in return. Instruct them to write down in their journal how it made them feel. Have them share their responses with the group.

4. Divide initiates into groups of three and ask them to come up with a community service project such as: a food or clothing drive, a neighborhood clean-up, answering phones for a telethon, etc. Have each group come up with a plan for carrying out their service projects. Give appropriate feedback and offer action steps to help them get started.

5. Distribute the construction paper, glitter, gift boxes and ribbon. Ask each initiate to create a gift certificate and a decorative box. Have her place the gift certificate in the decorative box as a reminder of the gift that she is about to give herself – the gift of giving. Explain how giving keeps the cycle of reciprocity constant in our lives.

6. Reiterate the benefits of community service and ask initiates if there is anything they would like to share before the session ends.

Suggested Topics

Following are suggested topics for continued work in the area of collective work and responsibility.
Dealing with Negative Peer Pressure, Beautifying the Community
Community Advocacy and Activism

Topic_____

Objectives

_____
_____
_____

Materials

_____
_____

Process

_____
_____
_____
_____
_____
_____
_____
_____
_____
_____
_____
_____
_____
_____
_____
_____
_____
_____
_____

Session Area 4.

Cooperative Economics

The Nguzo Saba defines cooperative economics as: to build and maintain our stores, shops and other businesses and to profit from them together.

The sessions in this area are designed to instill the principle of cooperative economics in initiates through career readiness, entrepreneurship, and money management.

Wealth Is A State of Mind

Objectives
To help initiates learn that true wealth begins in the mind. To help initiates explore their feelings about money.

Materials
Flipcharts, copies of the book "How to Think Like a Millionaire" by Mark Fisher and Marc Allen, pens and paper

Process
1. Briefly go over the objectives for this session.
2. Introduce the activity by asking initiates to write down what they believe to be the beliefs and habits of the wealthy. Have initiates share their responses with the group. Give appropriate feedback. Ask initiates to read pages 135-138 of "How to Think Like A Millionaire" and compare their responses with the principles outlined in the book.
3. Ask the group the following questions.
   - What is your greatest fear when it comes to money?
   - What messages did you receive about money growing up?
   - What are you family's beliefs about money?
   - What do you think wealthy people do with their money?
   - What do you think poor people do with their money?
   - When you get money what is the first thing you do with it and why?
   - What small step can you take to develop wealthier beliefs and habits?
4. Point out that true wealth is not about how much money one has, but how one lives his/her life. It begins in the mind then extends to the purse.
5. Reiterate the principles covered on pages 135-138 of "How to Think Like A Millionaire"
6. Ask initiates if there is anything they would like to share before the session ends.

Developing A Prosperity Plan

Objectives
To help initiates take charge of their financial future. To help initiates identify action steps that they can take to better manage their money.

Materials
Flipchart, notepads and pens

Process
1. Briefly go over the objectives for this session.
2. Introduce the activity by stating, "There isn't an aspect of our lives that is not affected by money. It affects where you live, how quickly you achieve your goals, and what type of lifestyle you are able to enjoy. The time to start planning for your financial future is now so that you can live comfortably as you grow older."
3. Tell initiates that the first step in developing a prosperity plan is knowing how you spend your money. Give each initiate a notepad and tell her that she is going to use the notepad to keep track of her spending habits. Instruct initiates to date a page each day, write down what they bought and how much it cost, starting with today. Tell them that this will give them a clearer picture of how they spend their money. After initiates have completed the page for today ask the following questions.
   - Were you surprised to find out how much you spent today?
   - Is this typical of your spending habits?
   - What do your spending habits tell you about yourself?
4. Introduce the four-step budgeting process: identifying your income, identifying expenses, totaling your income and expenses, setting up a spending and savings plan. Create a sample budget on the flipchart and go over it with initiates.
5. Stress the importance of living within your means and saving a portion of your income.
6. Conclude the session by discussing the principle of tithing (giving back a tenth of all the money you receive and regularly donating it to a spiritual institution or an organization that helps those who are less fortunate than you). Explain to initiates that giving is what keeps the cycle of abundance flowing in our lives.
7. Ask initiates if there is anything they would like to share before the session ends.

What Am I Good At?

Objective
To help initiates identify their skills and talents.

Materials
Newsprint, markers

Process
1. Briefly go over the objective for this session.
2. Introduce the session by saying, "Everyone has a special talent." "Everyone has a gift to offer. By uncovering your gifts you will be better able to set career goals."
3. Divide initiates into three groups. Give each group a sheet of newsprint and ask them to talk about their skills, talents and hobbies. Ask them to compose a group talent sheet listing the groups' skills, hobbies and talents. Have each group share their talent sheet and give appropriate feedback.
4. Instruct participants to go back to their groups and discuss their career aspirations. Ask group members to provide each person in their group with two action steps that they can take to move closer to their career goals. Have each group report out to the larger group. Give appropriate feedback.
5. Conclude the session by reiterating that everyone has a special talent and once we discover it we have a responsibility to nurture it.
6. Ask initiates if there is anything they would like to share before the session ends.

Exploring Career Options

(Field Trip to a Career Fair)

Objective
To help initiates learn about the different career options that are available to them.

Material
Notepads and pens

Process
1. Explain to initiates that the purpose of attending the career fair is to explore their career options.
2. Instruct participants to network in pairs and collect information about the various companies that are represented at the career fair.
3. Tell participants to jot down which companies left the greatest impression on them and why?
4. At the end of the field trip, tell initiates that a guest speaker will be coming in next week to discuss entrepreneurship.
5. Ask initiates if there is anything they would like to share before they leave.

Exploring Entrepreneurship
(Guest Speaker)

Objectives

To help initiates learn about entrepreneurship. To help initiates consider entrepreneurship as a possible career choice.

Materials

Journals, pens, copies of the book "In Her Footsteps" by Annette Madden.

Process

1. Briefly go over the objectives for this session.
2. Introduce the concept of entrepreneurship by discussing some of the successful Black Women who are highlighted in the book "In Her Footsteps."
3. Ask the following questions.
   - What similarities do the women who we've discussed have? How are they different?
   - What does it take to be a successful female entrepreneur?
   - Why is it important for African-Americans to support Black owned business?
4. Introduce the guest speaker and leave time for initiates to ask her questions.
5. Ask initiates if there is anything they would like to share before the session ends.

Note

You should try to secure a guest speaker one month ahead of time. Your guest speaker should be: an African-American woman business owner or an African-American woman who runs an entrepreneurship program.

Suggested Topics

Following are suggested topics for continued work in the area of cooperative economics.
African-American Youth and Consumerism, Investment Strategies and How to Open A Bank Account

Topic_____

Objectives

_____
_____
_____

Materials

_____
_____

Process

_____
_____
_____
_____
_____
_____
_____
_____
_____
_____
_____
_____
_____
_____
_____
_____
_____
_____
_____
_____

Session Area 5.

Purpose

The Nguzo Saba defines purpose as: to make our collective vocation the building and developing of our communities in order to restore our people to their traditional greatness.

The sessions in this area are designed to instill the principle of purpose in initiates through the promotion of personal mission statements, goal setting and values-clarification.

Knowing What's Important

Objectives
To help initiates clarify their values. To help initiates develop a value-system that promotes responsible decision making.

Materials
Pens and paper

Process
1. Briefly go over the objectives for this session.
2. Ask initiates to write the question, " what's important to me?" and have them jot down every thing that comes to mind. Have initiates share their responses with the entire group and give appropriate feedback.
3. Explain to initiates that they have just created a list of their values. Define the word "value" and discuss the importance of being clear about your values.
4. Discuss what sorts of things can happen when people are not clear about their values, then ask initiates to review their values list and write down next to each value whether the value is helping them to make smart decisions and reach their goals or hindering them. Have initiates share their responses with the group. Ask the group to suggest steps that each initiate can take to move towards a value system that would enable her to make better decisions and reach her goals.
5. Conclude by stressing the importance of being clear about what's important to you.
6. Ask initiates if there is anything they would like to share before the session ends.

Figuring Out Your Purpose

Objectives
To help initiates develop a sense of purpose. To introduce initiates to the concept of a personal mission statement.

Material
Flipchart, journals and pens

Process
1. Briefly go over the objectives of this session.
2. Ask initiates to define the word "purpose" Record their responses on the flipchart and give appropriate feedback.
3. Explain that everyone has a purpose in life and knowing one's purpose enables one to live by their values and set goals for their lives.
4. Explain that you will be taking the group through a series of questions to help them begin to figure out their purpose. Ask the following questions and instruct the group to respond in their journals.
   - Why are you here?
   - What purpose were you created to serve?
   - How are other people better off as a result of knowing you?
   - What are you good at?
   - What do others say that you're good at?
   - What excites you about the world?
   - What makes you angry about the world?
   - What would you like to change about the world and why?
   - What do you want to contribute to the world and why?
   - What makes you happy?
5. Ask the group to share their responses and give appropriate feedback.
6. Explain the concept of a personal mission statement (a sentence that sums up why you are here and what you intend to do with your life).
7. Explain that all successful organizations have a mission statement which sums up why the organization was formed and what purpose it intends to serve. Explain that people, just like organizations need to have mission statements to give them a sense of clarity and focus.
8. Explain to initiates that a good mission statement should be clear and action-oriented. For examples of mission statements pick up a copy of the book "The Path" by Laurie Beth Jones.
9. Give initiates about 15 minutes to begin working on their mission statements and have them share their mission statements with the group. Share positive observations and encourage the group to do the same.

10. Tell them that a good mission statement takes time and they will go through many drafts before completing it. Ask initiates if there is anything they would like to share before the session ends.

11. Ask initiates to bring in personal keepsakes and mementos for the next session.

Mapping Out My Goals

Objectives
To help initiates formulate and write down their goals. To show initiates how to create a visual representation of their goals.

Materials
Newsprint, markers, journals, assorted magazines, glue, scissors, and initiates' keepsakes.

Process
1. Briefly go over the objectives for this session and explain that this will be a two-part session.
2. Discuss the concept of goal setting and explain that goals are like roadmaps in that they guide you and give you a point of focus. Explain that goals enable us to think beyond today and assume greater control over our lives.
3. Talk about S.M.A.R.T goals (goals that are small, measurable, achievable, realistic and time-driven). Explain how setting S.M.A.R.T goals allows us to map out the necessary steps to get where we want to go.
4. Distribute the journals and ask initiates to jot down a few words describing what they would like to achieve, accomplish and contribute in life.
5. After about twenty minutes have initiates share their goals with the group and share your positive observations.
6. Distribute a piece of newsprint and a marker to each initiate. Ask them to divide their newsprint into the following categories: personal life, friendships, spiritual life, character development and contributions to humanity. Introduce the concept of a goal map explaining that it is a visual method of mapping out one's goals. Instruct them to begin working on their maps, starting with the personal life category. Ask initiates to look through the magazines and cut out pictures, words, and images that represent what they want to achieve, accomplish and contribute in their personal lives. Tell them that they can place pictures of themselves, mementos and anything else that represents who they are and where they want to be in this category. In this category they can also include skills, hobbies and talents that they want to enhance, or develop.
7. After completing the personal life category have them stop and answer the following questions.
   - What did this exercise teach you about yourself?
   - What did you learn about the other group members?
   - What category do you want to work on next and why?
8. Conclude by reiterating the importance of setting goals. Tell them that they will continue working on their goal maps at the next session.

Mapping Out My Goals *(Part 2)*

Objectives
To help initiates articulate their goals. To enable initiates to continue to create a visual representation of their goals.

Materials
Goal maps from last session, journals, magazines, glue, scissors

Process
1. Briefly go over the objectives for this session.
2. Instruct initiates to work on their goal maps for about 30 minutes.
3. At the end of the allotted time period, have initiates explain their goal maps to the group and give positive feedback.
4. Explain to initiates that they will need to work on their goal maps continually, because as their needs change so will their goals. Tell initiates that they can create additional categories if they want to.
5. Wrap up the session by discussing the following questions.
   - What are you aware of now that you didn't realize before?
   - How can you use your goal map as a foundation to help you reach your goals?
6. Ask initiates if there is anything they would like to share before the session ends.

Affirming Your Success

Objectives
To help initiates affirm their success. To help initiates realize that they can learn from failures and mistakes.

Materials
Paper and Pencils

Process
1. Briefly go over the objectives for this session.
2. Start the session by asking initiates, "who has control over your success?" Give appropriate feedback.
3. Ask initiates to identify a situation where they felt like they failed and write it down. Have initiates pair up and share their responses. Ask initiates to identify a situation where they felt successful and write it down. Have each initiate give the other supportive feedback
4. Ask initiates to write down what they learned from both experiences and have them share what they've learned with the group.
5. Ask the following questions.
   - Do our past failures determine what happens to us in the future? Why or why not?
   - How can failures be useful as tools for success?
   - When do you feel most successful?
   - What can you do to affirm your success?
6. Conclude by having initiates recite a positive affirmation.
7. Ask initiates if there is anything they would like to share before the session ends.

Suggested Topics

Following are suggested topics for continue work in the area of purpose. Time Management, Creative Visualization, Community Building and Organization Skills

Topic _____

Objectives

_____
_____
_____

Materials

_____
_____
_____

Process

_____
_____
_____
_____
_____
_____
_____
_____
_____
_____
_____
_____
_____
_____
_____
_____
_____
_____
_____
_____

The Nguzo Saba defines creativity as: to do as much as we can in the way that we can in order to leave our community more beautiful and beneficial than we inherited it.

Since this session area focuses on creativity, I have provided you with session topics, objectives and recommended resources, but I left the process and content up to you. This way you will be able to practice the principle of creativity.

This session area is designed to instill the principle of creativity in initiates through the cultural arts and through learning about African-American history.

African Hairstyles and Fashion

Objectives

To help initiates learn about traditional African fashions and hairstyles. To help initiates understand the techniques that our ancestors used for assembling clothing and wearing headwraps *(geles)*.

Recommended Resources

- Belfer, N. (1992) Batik and Tie Dye Techniques New York: Dover Publications
- Picton, J and Mack, J. (1993) African Textiles, London: British Museum Press
- Thomas-Osborne, V. (1982) Traditional and Contemporary Hairstyles for the Black Woman, Col-Bob Associates

Process

_____
_____
_____
_____
_____
_____
_____
_____
_____
_____
_____
_____
_____
_____
_____
_____
_____
_____
_____
_____
_____
_____
_____
_____
_____
_____

African Dance and Music

Objectives
To help initiates learn traditional African dance movements. To help initiates learn about traditional African music.

Recommended Resources
- Assante, K. (1996) African Dance: An Artistic Historical and Philosophical Inquiry. Trenton: Africa world press
- (Video on traditional African dance and music)

Process

_____
_____
_____
_____
_____
_____
_____
_____
_____
_____
_____
_____
_____
_____
_____
_____
_____
_____
_____
_____
_____
_____
_____
_____
_____

African History

Objective
To help initiates to learn about traditional African civilizations.

Recommended Resources
- Diop, C.A (1974) The African Origin of Civilization, New York: Lawrence Hill.
- (Video of the movie "Shaka Zulu")

Process

_____
_____
_____
_____
_____
_____
_____
_____
_____
_____
_____
_____
_____
_____
_____
_____
_____
_____
_____
_____
_____
_____
_____
_____
_____
_____
_____
_____
_____

African-American History

Objectives
To help initiates learn about the struggle that their ancestors endured in order to make a better life for future generations. To help initiates learn about the contributions that African-Americans made to America.

Recommended Resources
- Miles, J. & Davis, J. (2001) Almanac of African Americans. New Jersey: Prentice Hall Press
- Morton, J.O & Morton, L.E. (1995) A History of the African American People, New York: Smithmark

Process

_____

_____

_____

_____

_____

_____

_____

_____

_____

_____

_____

_____

_____

_____

_____

_____

_____

_____

_____

_____

_____

_____

_____

_____

_____

_____

_____

_____

_____

African-American Food and Social Etiquette

Objectives

To help initiates learn about the African-American cultural traditions as they relate to food and social etiquette. To help initiates learn how to properly set the table and conduct themselves at a formal diner.

Recommended Resources

- Ford, C. (1988) Guide to Modern Manners. New York: Crown Publishers
- Copage, William. An African American Celebration of Culture and Cooking, Morrow Publishers

Process

_____
_____
_____
_____
_____
_____
_____
_____
_____
_____
_____
_____
_____
_____
_____
_____
_____
_____
_____
_____
_____
_____
_____
_____
_____

Suggested Topics

Following are suggested topics for continued work in the area of creativity. African-American Dolls and Quilt Making, Popular Dance and Music and Decorating.

Topic_____

Objectives

_____

_____

_____

Materials

_____

_____

_____

Process

_____

_____

_____

_____

_____

_____

_____

_____

_____

_____

_____

_____

_____

_____

_____

_____

_____

_____

_____

_____

_____

_____

The Nguzo Saba defines faith as: to believe with all our heart in our people, our parents, our children, our teachers, our leaders, and in the righteousness and victory of our struggle.

For the purposes for this session area I would like to offer you a broader definition of faith (spiritual assurance). The sessions in this area are designed to help initiates discover how spirituality can be incorporated into their daily lives.

What Is Spirituality?

Objectives
To help initiates determine for themselves what spirituality means to them. To help initiates figure out how to develop a personal relationship with God in a way that is meaningful to them.

Materials
Journals and pens

Process
1. Briefly go over the objectives for this session.
2. Start out by explaining the difference between spirituality and religion. Tell initiates that you will not focus on a specific religion or particular spiritual practice, instead the group will discuss what spirituality means to each person in the room.
3. Ask initiates, "what is spirituality?" Have them respond in their journals. Ask initiates to share their responses with the group and share positive observations.
4. Ask initiates to think about a powerful spiritual experience that they had and how it changed their life. Ask initiates to tell the group about their experience and give appropriate feedback.
5. Explain to initiates that you will be leading them through a discussion designed to help them figure out how they see and experience God. Ask the following questions.
   - Who is God to you?
   - How do you experience God's presence?
   - How does it feel when you are in God's presence?
   - How do you communicate with God?
   - How do you acknowledge God?
   - How do you show others that you are a child of God?
6. Share positive observations and conclude this segment of the session by saying, *Spiritual growth is just as important as mental and emotional growth. The more we know about our spiritual beliefs, the better able we will be to incorporate them into our daily practices.*
7. Conclude with a visualization, meditation or prayer.
8. Ask initiates if there is anything they would like to share before the session ends.

Gratitude Lists

Objective
To help initiates recognize the many ways that they are blessed.

Materials
Journals and pens

Process
1. Briefly go over the objective for the session.
2. Explain the concept of gratitude and ask initiates to define what gratitude means to them.
3. Ask initiates to write down in their journal at least twenty things that they are grateful for. This exercise may take some time, but let initiates struggle through it until they come up with twenty things.
4. When they are finished, have them share their gratitude lists with the group. Give appropriate feedback.
5. Conclude with a visualization, meditation or prayer.
6. Ask initiates if there is anything they would like to share before the session ends.

Experiencing Beauty and Sacredness

(Field Trip to A Garden)

Objective
To help initiates realize that beauty exists in all of God's creations.

Materials
Journals and pens

Process
1. Explain the purpose of this field trip.
2. Instruct initiates to take in all of their surroundings and look for patterns, creations and objects that inspire and soothe them. Have initiates jot down their thoughts in their journals. Go to a private area in the garden and ask initiates to share their discoveries. Give appropriate feedback
3. Conclude by reciting a poem that deals with beauty, creation or nature.
4. Ask initiates if there is anything they would like to share before they leave.

Building Courage

Objectives
To help initiates trust their intuition. To help initiates build courage

Materials
Flipchart, journals and pens

Process
1. Briefly go over the objectives for the session.
2. Ask, "what makes a person courageous?" and record the group's responses on the flipchart. Give appropriate feedback.
3. Ask the following questions and instruct the group to respond in their journals.

- Recall a time when your intuition told you to do something and you listened. What happened? Recall a time when you did not listen to your intuition. What happened?
- If you could do anything you wanted what would it be and why?
- If you were ten times bolder what would you be doing?
- Recall a time you took a risk and you were pleasantly surprised by your courage?
- What can you do today to build up your courage?

4. Give appropriate feedback. Conclude with a scripture or reading that deals with courage.
5. Ask initiates if there is anything they would like to share before the session ends.

Making Everyday A Spiritual One

Objectives
To help initiates learn that everyday is sacred and special. To help initiates realize that they can honor God daily by how they live their lives.

Materials
Newsprint, and markers

Process
1. Briefly go over the objectives for the session.
2. Ask initiates, "How can we make everyday a spiritual one?" and record their responses on the flipchart. Give appropriate feedback.
3. Divide initiates into three groups and have each group draw a house on a piece of newsprint. Explain that the house symbolizes the inner house of their heart. With this idea in mind, tell them to build an extension to the house that represents the many ways that they can honor God in their daily lives. For example, they can add a garden to represent how they honor beauty. Or, they can add a porch to represent how they honor discussion time with God. Encourage initiates to be creative.
4. Have each group explain their house and provide positive feedback.
5. Conclude with a prayer, meditation or visualization.
6. Ask participants if they would like to share anything before the session ends.

Suggested Topics

Following are suggested topics for continued work in the area of faith. Forgiveness, Trust, Community Spirit, Faith as it relates to African-Americans Enduring and Overcoming Slavery, and Faith as it relates to the Civil Rights Movement

Topic_____

Objectives
_____
_____
_____

Materials
_____
_____
_____

Process
_____
_____
_____
_____
_____
_____
_____
_____
_____
_____
_____
_____
_____
_____
_____
_____
_____
_____
_____

A Final Note to the Facilitators

There are additional subject areas that you may want to consider covering such as: Sexuality, Sex Education, Hygiene, Gynecological Care, Breast Exams, Proper Nutrition and Diet and Holistic Health Care. Remember, it's your program, so structure it to meet your needs.

Don't be discouraged if you were not able to cover all of the sessions. What is most important is, that initiates develop a basic understanding of the principles of Nguzo Saba and how to incorporate them into their lives.

8

Planning and Organizing the Initiation Retreat and Crossover Ceremony

The Initiation Retreat

The initiation retreat is a major component of the African-centered rites of passage program. It reinforces the tradition of youth being taken out of the village to prepare themselves to crossover. Initiation retreats can be carried out in a number of ways. You can choose to hold a weekend retreat, an overnight retreat or a one-day retreat. This guidebook offers suggestions for planning and organizing a weekend retreat. However if you are offering a condensed version of the program, you can modify the suggested retreat planning and implementation steps.

You should begin planning the initiation retreat about four to six months in advance. This allows ample time for developing a theme, planning the agenda, visiting retreat sites, securing space and handling all of the other details that are sure to arise.

Whenever I conduct train-the trainer workshops on how to develop a rites of passage program, I get a lot of questions around planning and organizing the initiation retreat. Following are the most commonly asked questions along with my responses. You can use this as a guide for your initiation retreat.

What is the significance of the initiation retreat?

The initiation retreat is representative of the initiation rituals and activities that are practiced in traditional African cultures. It is a testing time where youth are separated from their village so that they can participate in a series of rituals and demonstrate their newly acquired skills and lessons. Initiation comes from the Latin root word *initiare*, which means to begin or to admit into membership as with ceremonies or ritual.

At what point in the rites program should I hold the retreat?

The initiation retreat should be held two to four weeks before the crossover ceremony. The initiation retreat signifies that the initiates are preparing themselves to crossover into young womanhood. Holding the retreat two to four weeks before the crossover ceremony gives initiates enough time to go over their lessons, practice the skills that they were taught and complete any supplementary work that your program may require.

How far in advance should I start planning the retreat?

I generally recommend four to six months in advance because you will need ample time to obtain funding unless you already have money for it, secure a retreat site and you will need to visit several places in order to find the retreat site that is right for you. You will also need time to plan your theme and agenda. I also recommend that you plan the crossover ceremony at the same time. This makes the planning process easier.

What steps are involved in planning the retreat?

Here are some of the steps involved in planning the initiation retreat.

- Step 1. Form your Intention

Figure out what you are seeking from the initiation retreat. What do you want the girls to demonstrate? What do you want the girls to get out of this retreat? What do you want them to leave the retreat knowing and feeling? The clearer you are about your intention, the better able you will be to develop rituals and activities that are in line with your purpose.

- Step 2. Decide On a Theme and Write Down The Kinds of Activities You Would Like to Provide.

Sit down with your committee and decide on a theme for the retreat. The theme is the main topic or focal point of the retreat. It provides attendees with direction and it indicates your purpose. The theme should be a short, catchy, phrase that sums up the purpose of your retreat. The theme should appear on the flyer and all correspondence related to the retreat. For example, a theme that I used for an initiation retreat was "The path to womanhood." After you have decided on a theme, start writing down the kinds of activities that you would like to provide. Will you offer experiential activities that reinforce what initiates have learned throughout the year? Will you offer sister-bonding activities that cultivate relationship building skills? Will you ask initiates to conduct workshops in order to demonstrate they have learned your key concepts? Will you ask initiates to create a skit focusing on a historical event in African-American history?

- Step 3. Prepare a Budget

Write down everything you think you will need for the retreat and estimate how much it will cost. This will enable you to get an idea of how much you can realistically offer.

- Step 4. Look for a Retreat Site

Once you have decided on the theme, activities and how much money you're working with, the next step is to look for a retreat site. The retreat site can be: a bed and breakfast, camp retreat center, dude ranch, a cabin or an elder's home. It is important to look for space early so that you can comparison shop. Also, visit each site to make sure that the setting is conducive to your needs. Don't depend on the retreat brochure. The facility almost always looks better in the brochure than it does when you actually arrive. Once you have decided on a retreat site you should book the space; otherwise you may find that you've planned a wonderful retreat but have no space to hold it in.

- Step 5. Meet with Initiates and Orientate Them
Although initiates already know that they will be participating in an initiation retreat, you should still tell them what to expect and what is required. Since the initiation retreat is a time for testing and preparation, the elders should do most of the planning and preparation. However, you can ask initiates for suggestions and incorporate their ideas into the retreat.

- Step 6. Orientate Parents and Obtain Their Written Consent
Parents need to know the purpose of the initiation retreat and what their daughters will be doing. It is also important to have parents sign a consent form and any other documentation that your organization requires.

Who should attend the retreat?
Mothers may want to attend the retreat to support their daughters. You will need to determine whether or not it's appropriate for mothers to attend. Depending on the nature and set up of your program, you will need to decide who would be the most appropriated people to attend the retreat. If you are a group of mothers providing a rites of passage program for your daughters, then it is appropriate and essential that you attend the retreat. However if you are an organization providing a rites of passage program for other people's daughters, then you will need to meet with your committee to determine who should attend, and make sure that parents are clear about where you stand on this issue and why.

What kind of rituals and ceremonies should we perform?
There are simple rituals that you probably perform already without calling them rituals. You may perform certain practices around the holidays. You might go to a special place when you write in your journal, meditate or pray. Rituals may be repeated often or they may be one-time acts. In the context of an African-centered rites of passage program; a special song, dance or wrapping the head with African fabric can be a ritual. What is most important is that the act or acts that you create and perform signify something meaningful for the group and that it enables participants to either connect, heal, bring closure, open, center themselves and bring a sense of sacredness to their lives.

The Crossover Ceremony

The crossover ceremony is the highest point of the African-centered rites of passage program. Parents, friends, family and other key people are invited to partake in this event. Traditionally, in an African-centered rites of passage crossover ceremony the audience members are also participants. Therefore, it is important to choose a space that allows for maximum participation. Since the audience is expected to participate in the ceremony, this should be made clear on the invitations. It is important to decorate the space in an African motif that utilizes a black, red and green color scheme. Food should be served directly following the program and the meal should comprise of traditional African and African-American dishes. Most books on Kwanzaa, offer a variety of recipes that are appropriate.

Since the ceremony is a very significant event, it's a good idea to have someone videotape it. You may want to notify community newspapers and find out if a reporter would be willing to cover the ceremony. Throughout the rites program you should have someone taking pictures of special activities, field trips, and rap sessions and display these photographs on a collage for all to see. You may want to invite a guest speaker. Make sure that she understands the African-centered rites of passage process and that her speech is one of affirmation and empowerment.

Initiates, staff and mentors should wear traditional African clothing, since the rites of passage program is African-centered. You may also indicate on the invitation that the preferred dress code is African style clothing. This is optional for guest but it should be a requirement for initiates and rites of passage leaders.

The Ceremony Step-by Step

Step 1. The Day Before the Ceremony

Preparation begins 1 to 3 days before the actual ceremony. Initiates and elders should fast to begin their cleansing process. It is believed that fasting brings clarity to the mind and instills self-discipline. When deciding on what type of fast you want to partake in, it is important to consider everyone's health restrictions. The fast may consist of fruits and vegetables, abstaining from meat and poultry, abstaining from caffeine and sugar products. Or you can ask members to fast from the television, telephone or the computer chat room. The second preparatory act is the ritual bath. There are many ways that this bath is carried out within the context of ceremony. One way to incorporate the ritual bath is to provide participants with rose or lavender scented oil and candles and ask them to bathe with these items the morning of the ceremony. Ask them to say an affirmation as they are bathing such as: "Today I am crossing over into a new stage of life." Or, " Today marks the beginning of a new me."

You can also have them create their own affirmations that support the new transition they are about to make.

Step 2. Preliminary Preparations On the Day of the Ceremony

It is generally recommended that you hold the ceremony on a weekend afternoon or, on a Friday evening to allow ample time for the activities and reception. The ceremony should be no longer than two hours. Initiates and key staff should arrive at least two hours before the scheduled start time in order to get dressed and take care of any last minute details. Speakers and performers should arrive one hour before the scheduled time. About 30 to 45 minutes before the scheduled start time, initiates should go into a private room until it is time for them to come forth. Appropriate music should be playing in the background for people who arrive early.

Light refreshments should be set out and printed programs should be readily available. There should be hosts/hostesses to welcome people as they enter and direct them to the refreshments and the initiates display table.

While initiates are in their private room an elder can offer words of encouragement, lead them in a prayer or meditation, keep them calm, and provide last minute suggestions on how to properly conduct themselves for the ceremony.

Step 3. The Procession

The procession can be carried out in a number of ways. Some processions involve the entire audience, while others only involve rites of passage leaders and initiates. And others involve only the initiates. The procession marks the beginning of the ceremony and it signifies that the initiates are coming forth. Spiritual processional music is highly recommended. There should be no eating or talking at this time.

Step 4. Welcome and Opening

After the procession, initiates and rites of passage leaders should remain standing while the ceremony leader leads the group in a prayer, gives her opening remarks and provides an overview of the day's events.

Step 5. Presenting the Young Women to the Community

There are a number of ways that the young women can be presented to the community. One way is to have the ceremony leader ask the parents to come up to the floor with their daughters and present them to the community. She then leads a ritual where each parent takes his or her daughter by the hand and asks the community to welcome and bless her. Afterwards the parents join hands, form a circle around their daughters and offer their blessings.

Step 6. Passage Statements

This is the point in the program where the keynote speech is made (about fifteen minutes) initiates make their speeches (about two to three minutes per initiate) parents make their speeches (about two minutes) and a rites of passage leader is delegated to speak on behalf of the staff and organization. You can also choose to present awards at this time.

Step 7. Creative Expression

This is the point in the program where initiates can perform a dance that they've rehearsed, a group song, or one or two members can be elected to sing a song or recite a poem. It is important that rites of passage leaders ensure that all performances are appropriate for the occasion.

Step 8. The Passage Closing Ritual

This is the climax of the ceremony. This ritual signifies the passage from girlhood to womanhood and as such appropriate symbols and ceremonial tools need to be incorporated. There is no recommended closing ritual, because the ritual needs to be specific to the experiences of those involved in your program. Since this passage is symbolic, it is essential that the ceremony leader/leaders explain the purpose of the closing ritual. A prayer and, or responsive reading should be used. The entire audience should participate in this ceremony. Gifts should also be given to the initiates, as it symbolizes that they have achieved a new status. Closing remarks should be made by the ceremony leader/leaders and you can conclude with a song, preferable the Black National Anthem, "Lift Every Voice and Sing."

Step 9. The Reception

The reception is the time for welcoming, remembering, connecting and rejoicing. It should be marked by a bountiful feast and appropriate music.

Follow-up Activities for Graduates

In order to aid young women as they continue their journey, it is important that you put some follow-up activities into place. The young women have spent a great deal of time with each other. Therefore a certain amount of sister-bonding has taken place. This should be encouraged and continued. The young women may have also developed close, personal relationships with the elders in the program and these relationships should be supported as well.

Here are some suggested follow-up activities.

- Encourage the graduates to continue building their friendships with each other.
- Encourage the graduates to plan projects and special events together.
- Encourage the young women to keep in touch with staff and mentors.
- Sponsor periodic events for graduates.

- Ask graduates to speak at the orientation in order to provide insight to new initiates on what to expect.
- Ask graduates to be guest speakers during the rap sessions or invite them to co-lead a special workshop.
- Provide follow-up workshops on college preparation, careers, and anything else that may be of interest to graduates.
- Be available for continued mentoring and guidance.

9

Honoring Your New Passage

Many women, including me, honor and recognize everyone else except themselves. Realize today that by completing this guidebook you have embarked on a new passage experience. And when you successfully carry out your rites of passage program you and the other program leaders will have undergone another passage experience; which should be celebrated and honored.

Being a rites of passage leader is a very sacred undertaking, because you are being entrusted with the care, development and spiritual nourishment of young females. You will be at the forefront of a momentous and life-changing process. This should not be taken lightly, and neither should your new passage experience.

Few women realize how great they truly are. I believe the reason that many of us do not recognize and honor our greatness is because we are not used to defining success on our own terms and giving ourselves due credit for all of our accomplishments. An easy way to begin the process is to write down what you've learned, re-affirmed or how you've grown as a result of reading this guidebook or carrying out your rites of passage program. Then make yourself a promise: *Promise to honor the passages of your own life.* No more taking yourself for granted or dimming your inner light. Today and each day after, you will honor yourself and embrace growth and transformation.

Ceremony for Program Leaders To Honor Their New Passage Experience

Congratulations on successfully carrying out your rites of passage program. Be excited that you were able to come together with other women to prepare younger females for successful adulthood. Let your heart be filled with anticipation and gladness. This is a day for you and your sister-friends (the other rites of passage leaders) to celebrate. You will need the following items for this ceremony.

- Frankincense and Myrrh incense set up on a small table
- Green, black and red candles set up on a small table
- Ball of purple yarn
- A journal and a pen
- A small bell
- Soft meditation music or African percussive music

Play music in the background, light the candles and incense, and sit in a circle, either in chairs or on the floor facing the table with the candles and incense. Ring the bell three times to signify that the ceremony is about to begin. Ask everyone to close their eyes and take several deep breaths. As you breathe in allow positive energy to come into your being as you breathe out release all tension and negativity. Ask participants to do this several times until they feel relaxed, comfortable and peaceful.

Now read the following prayer aloud:

Dear God, we ask that you bless this space. We thank you for all that you have done in our lives and the lives of the young women who you entrusted us to guide. We call upon you in truth and in spirit and ask that you continue to guide as. We are open to receiving your knowledge now and in the future. This is a blessed day for it marks wonderful endings and new beginnings. We are so grateful that you've entrusted us with this sacred endeavor and all that we have received we will continue to multiply. We are your talented, and gifted children and with your guidance and blessings we are unstoppable. We know that you have a special plan and purpose for our lives and we pledge to do our part to bring your will for our lives into fruition. From this day forward, we walk with your wisdom and light. This is a momentous occasion, because today we are awakened women.

Have one participant extinguish the black candle and say. *"Thank you God for the dawning of a new experience."*

Have one participant extinguish the red candle and say. *"Thank you, God for strength, life and the creative gifts to manifest our dreams."*

Have one participant extinguish the green candle and say. *"Thank you, God for abundance and success beyond measure."*

Take out the ball of purple yarn and starting with yourself; let the yarn unravel until each person has a strand of it. Now say, *"At this moment we are all connected. Our linkage to this strand of yarn represents our connection to one another. As rites of passage leaders we have just went through our own passage experience. We have grown and our lives have been transformed. We will never be the same."* Then say, *"I am now going to cut the yarn and give each of you the strand that you are holding on to. Put your strand of yarn in a special place and keep it as a reminder of the passage we've made together."*

Ring the bell three times to conclude the ceremony and write down your desires for the coming year in your journals.

Journal Entries

In the next year, I see myself...................
It would make me joyously happy to ....
I would like to learn more about ....
I feel more empowered because ....
I am beautiful because ....
I give thanks for ....
I would like to improve my life by ....

Now go out and celebrate together!

Sample Letter to Parent/Guardian

Dear Parent/Guardian:

During this school year, XYZ organization will be offering a rites of passage program for girls and young women. About fifteen young ladies will be selected to participate in the program. A rites of passage program is an excellent way for young ladies to learn about their cultural heritage, learn and practice life skills, build positive self-esteem and build healthy relationships with their peers.

Your daughter has expressed an interest in participating in the program, which will be starting soon. Enclosed is a consent form and information about our organization and the rites of passage program. Your daughter has not been selected yet and will not be considered until you give your permission. This is a very special program and only a few girls will be selected to participate. Participation in the program is completely voluntary.

Please read the parent/guardian consent form thoroughly and return it by (date). If you have any questions or concerns please feel free to call us. We are in the process of scheduling a parent meeting so that we can provide you with more detailed information about the program and address your questions and concerns. A staff member will be contacting you soon to get an idea regarding the best day and time to schedule the meeting. Thank you for your time.

Sincerely

Your name
Title

Sample Parent/Guardian Consent Form

Your permission is requested for your daughter
_____ to participate in the rites of passage program at xyz organization. The rites of passage program will run from (date) to (date). A total number (number of group sessions, field trips and other activities) is scheduled. There are (number of components) that your daughter will be required to participate in which include: (name of component and frequency of meetings).

Your daughter will have the opportunity to learn and practice new skills and behaviors that will help her prepare herself for successful adulthood.

Because the program is based on building trusting relationships between initiates (your daughter) and rites of passage leaders, the rites of passage leaders will keep information shared by program participants confidential except in certain situations in which there is an ethical responsibility to limit confidentiality.

By signing this form I give my informed consent for my daughter to participate in the rites of passage program.

Parent/Guardian _____ Date_____
Parent/Guardian_____ Date_____
Daughter's Signature_____ Date_____

Return to (your name, title and address)

Dear Student:

XYZ organization will be starting the rap session component of the rites of passage program very soon. Rap sessions are a way for young ladies such as yourself to come together to address issues that affect their lives and talk about whatever is on their minds. Please tell us what topics you would like to learn more about or that you are interested in. Please put a check mark next to any subject that you think would be helpful for young ladies of today.

_____dealing with parents   _____ managing your money
_____learning to stand up for yourself   _____decision making
_____setting goals   _____ dating and relationships
_____making friends and building strong friendships
_____Improving your community   _____ sexuality

Other_____
_____

Comments
_____
_____

Fill in your name only if you want to be contacted about the rap sessions
Name_____ Date_____

Return to (your name, title and address)

Sample Volunteer Application Form

Name: _____

Address: _____

City:_____ State:_____ Zip:_____

Telephone. Home: _____ Work: _____

Employer: _____

Business Address: _____

City: _____ State:_____ Zip: _____

Occupation: _____

Length of time at your company: _____

Marital Status_____ Age range 25-35_____ 36-45_____ 46-59____ 60+_____

1. Why are you interested in volunteering with the XYZ rites of passage program?

2. What do you hope to contribute?

3. What do you hope to get out of volunteering with the XYZ rites of passage program?

4. What are your hobbies and special interests?

5. Tell us a little about yourself.

6. Tell us why you think you would make a good role model for African-American young women.

7. Please give us the names and telephone numbers of three people who can provide references for your personal and professional character

8. The XYZ rites of passage program requires a minimum commitment of (#of hours per month) for (# of months that your program will run) Can you give this much time? Yes_____ No_____

9. All potential volunteers are required to attend our orientation, which will be held on (date and time).

Please return this form to:

Sample Initiate Application Form

Personal Information

Name: _____

Address: _____

City:_____ State:_____ Apt.# _____

Home Phone#_____ Pager/Cell_____

Date of Birth:_____ Age:_____

Emergency Contact Person:_____ Phone#_____

Parent/Guardian Information

Name: _____

Address: _____

Relationship to you:_____

Address:_____

City:_____ State:_____ Zip: _____

Home Phone #_____ Job# _____

Place of Employment: _____

Educational Background

Name of School: _____

School Address: _____

Principal:_____ Guidance Counselor:_____

Grade:_____ Grade Average: _____

Hobbies and Personal Interests

List your hobbies and extracurricular activities.

_____

_____

Tell us why you would like to be part of the XYZ rites of passage program?

_____

_____

What do you hope to gain from participating in the program? What life lessons and skills do you hope to learn?

_____

_____

What do you have to offer the XYZ rites of passage program? How will the overall program benefit as a result of you being a part of it?

_____

_____

Who is your biggest role model and why?

_____

_____

What has been one of the most positive experiences in your life and what did you learn form it?

_____

_____

Suggested Reading

Echevarria, Pegine. <u>For All Our Daughters: How Mentoring Helps Young Women and Girls Master the Art of Growing Up</u> Worcester, Massachusetts: Chandler House Press, 1998.

Edward, Sims. <u>Rites of Passage Program for Black Youth</u> Philadelphia, Pennsylvania: B.F.R. Publications, 1976.

Fair, Frank. <u>Orita: for Black Youth: An Initiation Into Christian Adulthood</u> Valley Forge, Pennsylvania: Judson Press, 1977.

Guildings, Paula. <u>When and Where I Enter: The Impact of Black Women on Race and Sex In America</u> New York: Morrow, 1984.

Hare, Nathan and Hare, Julie. <u>Bringing the Black Boy to Manhood: The Passage</u> San Francisco, California: The Black Think Tank, 1985.

Hudson, Wade and Wesley, Wade. <u>Afro Bets: Book of Black Heroes from A to Z</u> Orange, New Jersey: Just Us Books, 1988.

Kaufer, Nelly and Osmer-NewHouse, Carol. <u>A Women's Guide to Spiritual Renewal</u> San Francisco, California: Harper, 1994.

Lewis, Mary. <u>Herstory: Black Female Rites of Passage</u> Chicago, Illinois: African American Images, 1988.

Mafori, Moore., Gilyard, Gwen., King, Karen and Warfield-Coppock, Nsenga. <u>Transformation: A Rites of Passage Manual for African-American Girls</u> New York: Stars Press, 1987.

McClester, Cedric. <u>Everything You Wanted to Know About Kwanzaa But Didn't Know Where to Ask</u> New York: Gumbs &Thomas, 1994.

Schiele, Jerome. <u>Human Services and the Afrocentric Paradigm</u> New York: Haworth Press, 2000.

Wright, Madeline. <u>Sisters Helping Sisters</u> Texas: Wheller Avenue Baptist Church, 1997.

About the Author

Since 1990, *Cassandra Mack, MSW* has worked with people from adolescence to middle adulthood and has helped them to develop the necessary tools to enhance their lives from the boardroom to the family room. From youth struggling through adolescence and learning to navigate tough issues to front-line employees and senior managers looking to fine-tune their workplace skills, Cassandra's programs provides those whom she works with, with practical strategies for achieving their desired results.

Cassandra Mack is president and lead trainer of *Strategies for Empowered Living Inc.*, a New York based consulting company that provides professional development training in the areas of: supervisory and leadership skills, youth development, the empowerment of girls and women in the workplace. Her mission is to help individuals and organizations accelerate their power, potential and productivity. She achieves her mission by speaking, teaching and writing about personal and professional empowerment.

Cassandra has conducted keynotes, break-out sessions and business seminars for regional, state and national conferences and conventions. Some of the organizations she has worked with include: *Xerox, TIAA-Cref, The National Mentoring Partnership, The Support Center for Nonprofit Management, Child Welfare League of America, Daniel Memorial Institute, National Resource Center for Youth Services, Big Brothers Big Sisters, Federation of Protestant Welfare Agencies, Covenant House, Department of Education, Archdiocese Drug Abuse Prevention Program, Wildlife Conservation Society, Empire State Coalition of Youth and Family Services* and *the Civil Service Employees Association.*

She is the author of six books. They are: *"Young, Gifted and Doing It: 52 Power Moves for Teens," "Smart Moves That Successful Youth Workers Make," "Her Rite of Passage: How to Design and Deliver A Rites of Passage Program for African-American Girls and Young Women," "Smart Moves That Successful Managers Make"* and *Cool, Confident and Strong: 52 Power Moves for Girls."* Her latest book, *"The Single Moms Little Book of Wisdom,"* is available at amazon.com and Barnes and Nobles bookstores.

Cassandra is the advice columnist for *Proud Poppa* magazine. She has a column in *The Harlem Parent* and has written articles for BELLE magazine, The New York Beacon and Guidelines. She was featured in the February 2007 edition of Black Enterprise. She's been a guest on Good Day New York, What Women Want, Teen Talk and numerous radio programs. She has received numerous awards for her work with youth including the National Association on Drug and Alcohol Problems Business and Labor Award and the New York City Housing Authority Tenant's Association Award for her work with youth in the Lower East Side Community. She's also been featured in The Network Journal.

Cassandra hosts a weekly online talk radio show under The New York Carib News entitled, *The No More Drama Hour of Power*. You can listen to her show via the internet by going to: *www.caribworldradio.com* Click on the on-demand-radio link.

Cassandra received her bachelor's degree from Brooklyn College and her Master's degree in Social Work from Hunter College.

Other Books By The Author

Cool, Confident and Strong: 52 Power Moves for Girls. ($12.95)
Give girls that tools they need to build healthy self-esteem and make smart dating and relationship choices. This book provides pre-teen and teenage girls with the tools they need to make decisions that respect their values and boundaries.

Young, Gifted and Doing It: 52 Power Moves for Teens. ($14.95)
Give your teenagers the tools they need to succeed with this success guide for teens. From resisting negative peer pressure to goal setting to developing a clear sense of purpose, this book provides teens with a basic blueprint that they can utilize to position themselves for lifelong success and achievement.

Smart Moves That Successful Youth Workers Make. ($24.95)
This book will show you how to become a highly effective youth worker. You'll learn: the seven roles of the front-line youth worker and how to manage each, how to avoid the ten most common mistakes that youth workers make and how to build assets in youth that have a lasting impact.

Her Rite of Passage: How to Design & Deliver A Rites of Passage Program for African-American Girls and Young Women. ($39.95)
This book will show you how to set up a rites of passage program from start to finish. It includes a 42-session workshop curriculum based on the principles of Kwanzaa and offers step-by-step guidelines for planning and carrying out an initiation retreat and crossover ceremony.

Smart Moves That Successful Managers Make. ($19.95)
This book will show you how to lead and manage more effectively. You'll learn how to: avoid the 12 most common mistakes that managers make, utilize mission-centered leadership, make office politics work for you, facilitate teamwork, manage up and bring out the best in yourself and your staff.

Here's A Book That Provides
Help, Hope & Healing **for Single Moms...**

Price: **$10.95**

The Single Moms Little Book of Wisdom

A new book by motivational speaker, author, women's empowerment coach, Cassandra Mack contains life-changing insight, empowering tools and practical advice for single mothers who are actively seeking ways to let go of the things that drain them, align their thoughts and habits with the things that bring joy, and live their best lives.

Addressing such issues as: surviving tough times, avoiding unnecessary drama, transforming yourself for greatness, getting serious about your success, practical prosperity, helping your children get what they need to thrive, escaping the superwoman trap, getting ready for real love and how not to be a bitter baby's mama. *The Single Moms Little Book of Wisdom,* is sure to be of great comfort and value to any woman whose journey has taken her to single motherhood.

You can purchase a copy of, *The Single Moms Little Book of Wisdom,* at: www.amazon.com or order it at any Barnes and Nobles bookstore. Discounts are available for Nonprofit organizations and large quantity orders by contacting the publisher directly, *iUniverse Inc.* at: 1-800-288-4677.

978-0-595-47036-5
0-595-47036-X

www.ingramcontent.com/pod-product-compliance
Lightning Source LLC
Chambersburg PA
CBHW080413290526

45791CB00008BA/2254